ENTREPRENEURS WILL SAVE THE WORLD

ENTREPRENEURS WILL SAVE THE WORLD

WHY THE BEST HOPE FOR OUR ECONOMY IS YOU

MICHAEL HYATT

MICHAEL HYATT & COMPANY
Franklin, Tennessee

Entrepreneurs Will Save the World

Bulk orders for your team? Email sales@michaelhyatt.com.
ISBN: 978-1-7353817-0-1

Printed in the United States of America
MichaelHyatt.com

CONTENTS

6
Join the Rescue
The Entrepreneurial Imperative

95

*In any real and living economy
every actor is always an entrepreneur.*

LUDWIG VON MISES, *Human Action*

1

WHO NEEDS ENTREPRENEURS?

*The Underappreciated Drivers
of Economic Growth*

Not long after I became the CEO of Thomas Nelson Publishers, I sent an email to my direct reports about replacing one standing meeting with another I thought more helpful. I copied all the executive assistants because I knew they would be the ones tasked with implementing the change.

One assistant replied all, thinking she was just replying to her boss: "Why does he keep changing things?" she said. "Can't he just leave well enough alone?" The short answer was no. I couldn't leave things alone. I knew they could be improved, and so I felt compelled to change them. Why? Because I'm an entrepreneur at heart. Entrepreneurs identify problems, solve them, and thereby drive the changes necessary for companies to flourish and economies to grow.

Maybe that's you. Welcome to the club! There are a lot of us. But as we'll see in this book, the truth is that our club needs more members. So, what if you don't consider yourself an entrepreneur? Let me challenge you to think differently. Maybe you need to start thinking of yourself as an entrepreneur, regardless of the position you are in now.

For years I thought the term *entrepreneur* applied just to business owners; it only fit people who built and led a company from the ground up. And, true enough, that's one definition of the word. But I've met many business owners who didn't seem very entrepreneurial at all.

I've also met corporate leaders, rank-and-file workers, even pastors I would describe as entrepreneurs. What gives? Well, it turns out there's another definition of *entrepreneur* worth considering. An entrepreneur is someone who sees a problem and risks time, money, reputation, or some other asset to deliver a solution for gain. I think of it as problem solving for a profit.

By that definition, you can be an entrepreneur in any kind of organization or industry, regardless of your position. Being an entrepreneur is less about your title and more about your mindset. It's how you approach life. Are you constantly seeing gaps that could be closed? Are you willing to stake something that matters on solving the problem for others? If so, you're an entrepreneur, and you're one of the key drivers to our economy's health and vitality.

Entrepreneurs see connections others miss and feel compelled to take action. We have a deep-seated belief that things can be better, that there's a solution for every problem, or at least a better tradeoff. We are restless, ambitious, and always looking for a way to improve the world we find.

Like Father, Like Son

My dad was always an entrepreneur. Every few years he'd start a new business. As it is with many entrepreneurs, this pattern was born of necessity.

Dad joined the Marines at age seventeen and fought in the Korean War. While on the battlefield, he suffered a significant head injury from a piece of flying shrapnel. He was in a coma for months and endured multiple surgeries, leaving him with chronic, lifelong pain and a permanent limp. This was back in the 1950s, long before the Americans with Disabilities Act protected disabled workers from discrimination in the workplace (and elsewhere). Employers were reluctant to hire the disabled.

Finally, his father-in-law gave him a job as an insurance salesman at his small agency. My dad immediately saw the potential in a position where his income was directly tied to his effort.

It wasn't long before he decided to strike out on his own. This led to a string of ventures: a life insurance agency, an oil exploration company, a fertilizer distributor, and a restaurant owner. None of these businesses succeeded the way he had hoped, so he'd launch something else, hoping this time he'd hit the big time.

Without question, I owe my entrepreneurial bent to my dad. Growing up, I watched him pour tremendous effort into each endeavor. I learned that business was about spotting a need and investing yourself in the solution.

I took his values and hard work ethic to heart. Whether I was a salesman on the front lines, a manager of a corporate department, an executive vice president with profit-and-loss responsibility, a CEO for a publicly held company, or an owner of multiple businesses of my own, I've always approached my role with the mindset of an entrepreneur.

Entrepreneurs are essential in any economy, whether in times of prosperity or decline. In fact, they're the best answer for periods of decline because their activity revitalizes the economy. Entrepreneurs are those who scout for opportunities and innovate, looking ahead to meet needs and make improvements. There will always be new problems to solve, and those solutions will result in new initiatives and companies that create jobs, help customers, and drive economic growth.

That's why I say entrepreneurs will save the world. It sounds grandiose, but consider the alternative.

A World Without Entrepreneurs?

Can you imagine a world without entrepreneurs? It's a pretty scary thought. Just think of the countless amenities, activities, and technological breakthroughs that exist today because an entrepreneur hit upon a new or better way of doing something: inexpensive food, medical technology, air-conditioned homes, digital tools, advanced communications, clean environments, leisure, accessible arts and entertainment, rapid travel, and more.

We count on these sorts of innovations to make life endurable, even enjoyable. And all these were made possible by entrepreneurs, the jobs they helped create, and the economic growth that compounded along the way as new entrepreneurs built on what had come before.

Imagine life in 1900. "No air travel, no antibiotics, no iPhone, no Amazon Prime, no modern high school and no air conditioning." That's how Michael Strain, director of economic policy studies at the American Enterprise Institute, painted just part of the picture. He then said, "Anyone who played down growth a century ago . . . would have been putting the existence of all these at risk by stifling, even marginally, the economic engine that allowed for their creation."[1]

Along the same lines, George Mason University economist Tyler Cowen offers a compelling thought experiment. He suggests we rerun American history from 1870 to 1990. This time, however, he says we should imagine what would happen if the US economy grew less each year than it actually did by just one percentage point. "In that scenario," he says, "the United States of 1990 would be no richer than the Mexico of 1990."[2]

Economic growth makes a real, concrete difference to the welfare and well-being of all of us. And entrepreneurs play a key part in that growth. It's true that big corporations play their part. But all those big firms started out small and grew because of the entrepreneurial drive of their founders. Outside large, dynamic firms, economic growth depends primarily on entrepreneurs and the changes they initiate.[3]

Entrepreneurs discover and invest in solutions. They then shoulder the risk to bring those solutions to people in need. And they do so for some sort of reward, usually monetary. Not all innovators are entrepreneurs, and not all entrepreneurs are innovators. Sometimes one person fulfills both functions, but they're different.

Inventors can create novel solutions to problems. But until they're mobilized in the marketplace, these solutions can't be distributed to those who need them. That's what entrepreneurs do. They're the bridge between needs and solutions. And they perform another essential function along the way. Not every solution works. By their willingness to risk failure, they help weed the market of poor or inadequate solutions.

Still, despite these essential functions, there's a stigmatization of entrepreneurs today. Instead of valuing entrepreneurs for their crucial contributions to bettering the world, pundits, politicians, and others seem happy to denigrate and devalue their role in society.

The Shame Game

In a 2014 essay, Rich Cooper of US Chamber of

Commerce Foundation expressed something I've felt for a long time now. "On the one hand," he says, "Americans have a long tradition of championing the entrepreneur, the underdog who strikes out alone and captures the American Dream. On the other hand, successful entrepreneurs today are facing hostile arguments that say their success makes them the bad guy."[4]

When you make money as an entrepreneur, there's an assumed obligation to "give back." It's like people can't imagine there's a difference in making money and taking it. So, it's incumbent upon someone earning a profit to give back, especially in the form of higher taxes. Anyone who doesn't happily go along with this way of thinking will be shamed into compliance.

This attitude is often fueled by individuals who have never operated so much as a lemonade stand. They rarely have the background or context to understand what entrepreneurs have at stake as they navigate complex business environments. Nor do they appreciate the enormous risks entrepreneurs take launching and sustaining a business, the pressure to find new markets, or the hard decisions that come with running a company. Business owners are presumed suspect. The message is, as one commentator put it, "If you're making too much money (however that's defined), then we don't like you and we don't trust you."[5]

There's no upside and plenty of downside when entrepreneurs are painted as the bad guys. The truth is entrepreneurs already "give back" by their very work. Let's say you employ 30 or 40 people; you're providing jobs and financial stability for individuals and families. Let's say you've created a new in-demand product; you're solving customer problems and meeting consumer needs. Let's say you've turned a profit; you're contributing to the economic growth of the entire community.

As an entrepreneur, you contribute to society in at least three ways:

1. Communities benefit from the jobs you provide and the growth you produce.

2. Governments (local, state, and federal) benefit through the taxes raised from your efforts.

3. Customers enjoy access to the goods or services you supply.

Everyone wins. The mere act of running a profitable business is giving. On the other hand, if entrepreneurs stop innovating and producing, then economic growth declines. And an economic downturn would ensue because jobs and investment from their enterprises would evaporate.

That's why we need more confident entrepreneurs,

not fewer. We should be applauding and celebrating entrepreneurship, not putting a vise grip on their activities or shaming them when they enjoy success.

Entrepreneurship is a social good. Helping your community by solving problems is virtuous. Making money and providing jobs is virtuous. Contributing to economic growth is virtuous.

Most entrepreneurs are fair-minded, hardworking people aspiring to build something of lasting value. They have a vision of an improved world, and they're not willing to wait for others to make it a reality. They take ownership to bring those improvements to the people who need them. That's why more entrepreneurs, not fewer, are the best hope for our economy.

Despite the labyrinthine regulations, licensing hurdles, limited access to capital, heavy taxation, and challenges of finding and keeping a skilled workforce, entrepreneurs provide two-thirds of all new jobs. Small businesses generate almost half the gross national product of the United States.[6]

Entrepreneurs are essential. As Ray Hennessey says, "If you truly believe in more jobs, in better wages and broader prosperity, you need Americans to innovate, to take risks, and put their capital at work to create new businesses. You should be rooting for their success, since the more money they make, the more profits they have to reinvest in their businesses. That reinvestment invariably creates jobs, which creates wealth for others."[7]

A Clarion Call

This entrepreneurial shame game couldn't come at a worse time. Entrepreneurialism is actually in decline around the world. And, added to the economic setbacks of the COVID-19 crisis, some entrepreneurs are suffering a crisis of confidence.

No wonder. Economic uncertainty can put us all on the fast-track to self-doubt. Given the risks they shoulder, entrepreneurs are especially vulnerable in downturns and disruptions. But, thanks to their resilience and resourcefulness, they're also the best equipped to answer a crisis when it comes.

That's why now more than ever we need entrepreneurs to step up and step out. Whether you're a dyed-in-the-wool entrepreneur or just someone entertaining the label for yourself, consider this book your clarion call.

Entrepreneurs Will Save the World is a manifesto for entrepreneurial engagement. More than that, it's a manual for economic growth. In the pages ahead, we'll explore the entrepreneurial mindset that helps generate growth (chapter 3). I'll reveal the various stages in entrepreneurial method (chapter 4) and share how entrepreneurs can respond in the midst of a crisis (chapter 5).

But before that, we'll look at the global decline in entrepreneurial activity (chapter 2). Given their essential role in economic health and vitality, it's essential to ask why they're disappearing and get a sense of what we can do about it. We'll turn to that now.

2

THEY'RE DISAPPEARING

Entrepreneurs Are Vanishing,
But There's Always Hope

American entrepreneurship is fading. It's a bummer to admit. I'm an entrepreneur, and I work with some of the best and brightest entrepreneurial leaders around through my BusinessAccelerator coaching program. As we saw in chapter 1, the contribution of entrepreneurs to economic growth—not to mention the greater societal good—is essential.

But it's true. The entrepreneurial engine that propels growth with new ideas, investment, and spunk is slipping. Economists, journalists, historians, and others are sounding the alarm. The headlines alone are enough to discourage:

- "Behind the Productivity Plunge: Fewer Startups"
- "The Mysterious Death of Entrepreneurship in America"
- "Start-Ups Aren't Cool Anymore"
- "American Entrepreneurship Is Actually Vanishing"
- "America's Startup Scene Is Looking Anemic"
- "The US Startup Is Disappearing"
- "Dynamism in Retreat"[1]

This isn't recent. By just one measure—the number of new companies—entrepreneurialism has been declining for decades in America. According to US Census Bureau data, the share of new startups as a percentage of overall businesses has fallen 44 percent since the late 1970s.[2]

And that's not the only metric of concern. Economist Wim Naudé notes several more: business entry and exit rates, patent filings, research productivity, new high-dollar jobs, and so on. The trendlines are all floating in the wrong direction. "The West's golden entrepreneurial and innovation age is behind it," he says. "Since the 1980s entrepreneurship, innovation and, more generally, business dynamics, have been steadily declining—particularly so in the US."[3]

And America isn't the only country experiencing a slump. Across the globe—even in places known for economic vitality—startups, patents, IPOs, and other indicators of vibrant enterprise are declining in number. Germany, Japan, Canada, South Africa, and Russia have all seen marked declines.[4] This regrettable decline in entrepreneurial activity comes at a time when entrepreneurs are needed more than ever before.

What's suppressing the entrepreneurial spirit? Speculation abounds, and some theories are better researched and documented than others. From what I can tell, there are at least six primary factors contributing to the problem here in the United States: onerous regulations, the impact of Big Business, funding challenges, demographic decline, shifting generational values, and age discrimination. Some of these problems have parallels in other countries.

I don't want to get in the weeds here, so I'll keep it short. But it's worth seeing what we're up against before we look more in depth at the traits and methods of entrepreneurs in coming chapters.

Wrapped Up in Red Tape

Managing around regulations can be a big challenge for entrepreneurs. They come with new ideas, after all, not necessarily lawyers. Yet there are applications, permits, fees, licenses, inspections, statutes, and more to worry about.

Entrepreneurs launching a new business often struggle to understand, let alone abide by, complex federal, state, county, and local codes. "Increased regulation, at both the state and federal levels, may be particularly burdensome for new businesses that lack well-staffed compliance departments," says *New York Times* writer Ben Casselman.[5]

And the rolls of red tape get longer every day. "A new regulation is promulgated in America roughly every two-and-a-half hours," says Ray Hennessey. "In fact, the cost of regulation in the U.S. is bigger than the economies of all but nine countries in the world."[6]

The civil liberties law firm, Institute for Justice, has released a series of reports on red tape in American cities. The reports examine barriers to entry in Baltimore, Maryland; Boston, Massachusetts; Chicago, Illinois; Houston, Texas; Los Angeles, California; Miami, Florida; Milwaukee, Wisconsin; Newark, New Jersey; Philadelphia, Pennsylvania; San Diego, California;

Seattle, Washington; and Washington, DC.[7]

"There are myriad laws on the books that make it difficult—sometimes even impossible—for people to start new enterprises," says Beth Kregor, introducing the institute's Chicago report. While some of the regulations might have been well intentioned, she points out that many were not. Regardless, the complex, interlocking system of codes and compliance amounts to a roadblock for entrepreneurs.

"Instead of a navigable system designed to make sure businesses meet reasonable health and safety standards," she says, "the overlapping rules of the city of Chicago and the state of Illinois create a matrix that is so confusing and nonsensical that it often seems designed to stop entrepreneurs in their tracks."[8] The same could be said for any of the cities and states mentioned.

Big Businesses, Big Impact

There's nothing wrong with Big Business as such. I'm for it. But, taken with the impact of other entrepreneurial dampeners, it's worth mentioning here.

To begin with, established companies possess many competitive advantages over startups: they've worked out the kinks in their business model, they're often better resourced, they can afford to lose money for a period to drive out competitors, and they can leverage their financial position to acquire startups, which in some cases stifles the energy of the smaller enterprise.[9]

Established companies can also use political influence to raise the regulatory fence and block competitors—big and small.

Beyond that, big companies suck entrepreneurial-minded employees out of the pool by hiring them. That can be helpful for those businesses, but it can have the effect of reducing their impact in the economy. Companies like 3M and Google provide a sandbox for enterprising employees to play in for as much as 20 percent of their time. Rather than charting their own course, they settle for a corporate gig where they can dabble with ideas while drawing a consistent paycheck. "Many of us suppress our entrepreneurial spirit and instincts in order to keep our jobs or our sense of security," warns Chris Ducker. "We do so at the expense of our own happiness, success, and fulfillment."[10]

Big Business also draws in potential entrepreneurs with perks they couldn't get on their own, at least initially. "Economists don't want to put these things into their models," says Brookings economist Ian Hathaway. "But I can tell you, as both an entrepreneur and a student debt holder, they absolutely factor into it."[11] I'm fine with companies hiring ambitious, entrepreneurial employees. But I wonder how often we factor what the tradeoff is costing the wider economy.

Funding Hurdles

Starting a business takes cash, sometimes a little, sometimes a lot. And the spigots don't flow as fast or full as they used to. Startups are finding it harder than ever to get funding.

The Small Business Administration says community banks provide 50 percent of all small business loans. But community banks have been closing at record numbers over the last 30 years. In the mid-1980s there were more than 18,000 FDIC-backed banks in the United States. Not even a third of that number are left today.[12]

Instead, banks have consolidated. Larger banks have scooped up smaller institutions. Unfortunately, big banks are not likely to give out small loans for startups. "Large banks," according to the US Chamber of Commerce, "are often unwilling to make loans under $100,000 because they're simply not profitable. This hurts the average startup founder, who only needs about $30,000 on average."[13]

There are other options, of course, including crowdfunding or borrowing money from your uncle. But alternate sources of funding have their challenges, too. "Fewer than 1 in 10 get 'angel funding' from someone wishing to help out," says Growthink president Dave Lavinsky, and "fewer than 1 in 100 advance to venture capital."[14] The sad reality is that without funding, lots of great business plans get dropped in the bottom desk drawer, while potential entrepreneurs take corporate jobs instead.

We're Running Low on People

Hard to believe, but it's true. When I was growing up, everyone was panicked about population growth. Paul Ehrlich published his runaway bestseller, *The Population Bomb*, in 1968. But his worst fears never materialized. Instead, much of the world is now having fewer children than ever.

To sustain existing populations, countries need a birth rate of just over 2. In the United States right now ours is 1.7, down from 3.6 in 1960. In Canada and the European Union, the average for both is 1.5, down from 3.8 and 2.6, respectively, in 1960.

What do babies have to do with business? Declining populations affect business on both the supply and demand side. "On the supply side, if you have fewer people, there are fewer companies being formed," explains Brookings economist Robert Litan. "On the demand side, a slowing population means less demand for new products."[15]

The Kauffman Foundation has expressed similar concern. "An aging population dramatically affects the pipeline of entrepreneurs," they say in their 2017 State of Entrepreneurship report, *Zero Barriers*, "and the slow labor for growth associated with it is connected to the long-term decline in entrepreneurial dynamism in the United States."[16] And that's not the only generational challenge on our hands.

Kids These Days

Millennials are the largest generation since the Baby Boomers, and they are paying a price for issues they didn't create. As we've seen, they started their careers on the tail end of the sharpest decline in new startups.

Most Millennials I know and deal with on a daily basis are incredibly creative and tenacious. But, as a cohort, they're trending the same direction as the numbers we've seen so far. "Although many millennials have an entrepreneurial mindset, fewer in this generation are starting their businesses before the age of 30 than their baby boomer counterparts were," according to a report in *Inc.*[17]

In fact, according to Federal Reserve data analyzed by the *Wall Street Journal*, business owners under 30 are fewer today than at any time in the last quarter century. Why? In the face of a challenging economic environment, they feel as though they don't have enough skills or experience, and so they opt for traditional employment, instead of branching out on their own.[18] Of course, you never really know if you're ready until *after* you try.

There's one more age-related answer for why we're seeing fewer entrepreneurs today. Given my age, it might seem like special pleading. But I think there's something to this, and it's worth noting.

Age Discrimination

Venture capital firm First Round Capital surveyed more than 500 US startup founders and discovered that investors' strongest bias is age. In fact, ageism is a bigger barrier than racism or sexism. Of those surveyed, "37% of founders believe startup investors' bias against founders based on age (compared to 28% on gender and 26% on race). A whopping 89% of respondents agree that older people face age discrimination in the tech industry generally."[19]

"The cutoff in investors' heads is 32," investor Paul Graham told the *New York Times Magazine*. "After 32, they start to be a little skeptical."[20] Graham was speaking of tech startups, but the bias seems to spread beyond Silicon Valley.

On some level, it's to be expected. Many of the biggest, splashiest entrepreneurs in the last several decades have been under 30:

Airbnb: Brian Chesky, 27

Apple: Steve Jobs, 21

Eventbrite: Julia Hartz, 27

Facebook: Mark Zuckerberg, 19

FUBU: Daymond John, 20

Groupon: Andrew Mason, 27

Instagram: Kevin Systrom, 26

Microsoft: Bill Gates, 20

Spanx: Sara Blakely, 27

Subway: Fred DeLuca, 17

WordPress: Matthew Mullenweg, 19

The media is fascinated with the kid-turned-entrepreneur narrative. It makes for a good headline. And I applaud and encourage entrepreneurism at any age. But contrary to popular opinion, the stereotype of cutting-edge, creative, energetic, and relentless kids dropping out of college to start a new venture just doesn't match reality.

Researchers at Duke and Harvard studied startups earning at least $1 million and discovered the founders' median age was 39. "Twice as many successful entrepreneurs are over 50 as under 25; and twice as many, over 60 as under 20," said Vivek Wadhwa, who led the research team. "In a follow-up project, we studied the backgrounds of 549 successful entrepreneurs in 12 high-growth industries," Wadhwa said. "The average and median age of male founders in this group was 40, and a significant proportion were older than 50."[21]

Despite these and other numbers, people assume that the young are the most likely to drive innovation and business growth. The result is that investors entrust money to untried executives, while the people with the most to contribute are assumed to have little left to offer. But of course they do. All entrepreneurs do.

Not the Last Word

The trends might be discouraging, but I refuse to let decline be the last word. Once identified, problems can be rectified—or at least ameliorated. The red tape problem can be addressed legislatively, or even in the judicial system as the Institute for Justice has done. When it comes to lower population growth, some governments are actually paying their citizens to have children. Another solution is importing more people, and immigrants have a good track record of packing entrepreneurialism in their luggage.

By far the best answer to all of the above challenges, however, is for existing entrepreneurs to double down and encourage more people to do the same. If you're already an entrepreneur, awesome! We need you. If you don't yet think of yourself as an entrepreneur, but you have a great idea, we need you, too! Entrepreneurs are the best hope for our economy.

The numbers don't lie, but they don't tell the whole story either. To say our best days of innovation and growth are behind us doesn't resonate with what I'm hearing from the entrepreneurs we work with at Michael Hyatt & Company, even in the 2020 downturn. Some are up, some are down, but they're not out. They're all hard at work trying to add value and solve problems for their customers.

That spirit of persistence is why I have hope, and why I believe you should too. Entrepreneurs are hardwired to cope with economic setbacks and uncertainty. We see opportunities where others see threats. Entrepreneurs know there must be a better way, and they're attuned to find it.

Here's an example of that spirit in action. Mike Lindell is the founder of MyPillow. With COVID-19 causing sleepless nights across the country, he spied an opportunity. Frontline medical and hospital workers needed personal protective equipment, specifically face masks.

In just three days, Lindell retooled his 200,000-square-foot factory to produce 10,000 cotton masks a day, using the tools and materials already on hand. Within a couple of months, he increased that to 50,000 and hired additional employees to meet the demand.

The crisis turned into an ongoing new product line for the company. As capacity increased, MyPillow started selling masks to the general public as well. "I want to be one of the manufacturers that stays out there," Lindell said.[22] Lindell's story illustrates several of the traits of the entrepreneurial mindset. And that's what we're covering next.

3

———

A BETTER WAY

8 Traits of the Entrepreneurial Mindset

Growing up with my dad was like entrepreneurial school. He taught me entrepreneurs determine their own income because the more stuff they sell, the greater the financial reward. He talked about the importance of being efficient, striving to improve conversions, and different techniques to sell stuff. I was inspired to give it a go. Dad told me I had the chance to shape my future by applying myself to something I loved and loved selling. He assured me I just needed to look for the right opportunity.

At age 11, I noticed a magazine ad promising to

send me a kit with boxes of all-occasion cards and suggestions on how to sell them at a profit. That seemed promising. If I could sell the cards, I could finally buy all the baseball cards, bubble gum, and dime magazines I wanted with my own money. Dad encouraged me to go for it. I filled out and mailed in the form. As I dropped it in the post, I imagined dollar bills crammed into my wallet.

Candidly, it was a bust. After calling on a few neighbors and getting lots of "no thanks," I didn't have the stamina to call on strangers. I hated being rejected and lacked resilience. At the time, I didn't understand that failure is baked into the entrepreneurial life. It's part of the process. So, I gave up for a couple of years.

My next entrepreneurial idea was to start my own lawn-mowing business. I saw other kids making money and figured I could do the same. I actually talked my dad into buying me a lawn mower. My pitch? If he would invest in the lawn mower, I'd be working all summer. He agreed. I didn't realize it at the time, but I was learning how to raise capital to start a business.

The bad news is that I bailed after about a month when I realized I actually had to do the hard work of acquiring customers and then executing the job. The good news was lawn mowing lasted longer than the cards. In fact, with each entrepreneurial venture I began, my ability to stick with something until I succeeded grew. It's fair to say tenacity ended up becoming one of my superpowers.

I don't think entrepreneurs are born, invent something, and then enjoy success. Entrepreneurship is more like learning to play a sport. You may have some natural talent, but the only way you really learn is by trying, failing, gaining resilience, problem solving, and applying yourself to fresh opportunities.

Being a lifelong learner has its benefits. I'm always reading, studying, exploring, trying out new ideas, and observing trends. There's nothing more valuable than learning from other leaders in the same or even very different fields. I'm constantly impressed with the breakthrough ideas by fellow entrepreneurs. I'm also constantly realizing areas I need to grow. And whenever I grow, my company does, too.

In chapter 1 I said being an entrepreneur is less about a role and more about mindset. This mindset allows entrepreneurs to paint the future with fresh possibilities and overcome obstacles. As I count them, there are eight traits of the entrepreneurial mindset essential to long-term success: openness, ownership, grayscale thinking, risk tolerance, resilience, resourcefulness, patience, and belief.

None of us are born with the full complement,

and none of us have developed them to perfection. There's no such thing. There's always room to develop and improve how we exercise these traits in our work on any given day. Wherever you're starting from, that ongoing development is essential to your long-term success. Let's begin unpacking the eight traits.

1. Openness

During the memorial service for Steve Jobs, his wife, Laurene Powell, noted Jobs's uncanny ability to be open to existing problems as well as open to future possibilities. "It is hard enough to see what is already there, to remove the many impediments to a clear view of reality," she said, "but Steve's gift was even greater: he saw clearly what was not there, what could be there, what had to be there. . . . He imagined what reality lacked, and he set out to remedy it."[1]

Entrepreneurs are uncannily open to opportunities. They see problems others don't. They get stuck on conundrums others ignore. They fixate on challenges others dismiss. They know that the answers to these sorts of problems could be products. As economist Israel Kirzner said, "Because the participants in this market are less than omniscient, there is likely to exist, at any given time, a multitude of opportunities that have not yet been taken advantage of. . . . To discover these unexploited opportunities takes alertness."[2] If entrepreneurs can solve for x, they will offer the world a gift and possibly profit for their trouble.

Canadian entrepreneur Mike Lazaridis, like Jobs, also had a knack for imagining what reality lacked. In 1999, years before Jobs invented the iPhone, Lazaridis invented the BlackBerry. By being open to new ideas, Lazaridis solved a major business communication problem by synchronizing a personal two-way pager with a company's email system so that business travelers had access to their corporate email regardless of their location.

In 2003, his company, RIM, really revolutionized how people work, by solving the problem of juggling two devices at once—a cell phone and a BlackBerry. The new BlackBerry became the first smartphone on the market. And the workforce has never looked back. In some regards, it's been a mixed blessing. Whether employees were in the office or not, they were connected. Regardless, it was a blessing, and productivity increased thanks to Lazaridis's vision.

Critics of entrepreneurs like Jobs and Lazaridis call them selfish or opportunists. I completely disagree. Entrepreneurs are the opposite of selfish. They're busy scouring the world solving problems that are not necessarily their own. Lazaridis put it this way: "We celebrate the risk-takers, the ones who stake it all on something nobody else sees . . . a few percent of the time you'd be making breakthroughs, because that's the other thing trailblazers do, they discover things that are utterly new."[3]

There's a difference between coping and solving, and that's why entrepreneurs are important. They're open to the better way—not only pining for it, but also pinpointing it and producing it—as opposed to just managing the broken pieces of our present reality. Entrepreneurs look for the gaps, holes, and bumps of our everyday lives and create ways of filling and smoothing the path for the rest of us.

Why do entrepreneurs solve problems? For the joy of it? Maybe. Out of curiosity or some sense of personal satisfaction? Sure. For money? That's a big part of it. To make their surroundings, community, or the world a better, more enjoyable place? Absolutely. All those reasons are valid because solving problems adds value and contributes to economic growth. And solving problems starts with the essential quality of openness—being open to problems and solutions alike.

2. Ownership

Entrepreneurs do not wait around for somebody else to solve the problems they observe. True entrepreneurs are compelled to find solutions. Ownership means they take the initiative.

Dan Haseltine, lead singer of the multiplatinum Grammy Award–winning band, Jars of Clay, exemplifies this ownership mindset. In 2001, while visiting Malawi on a mission trip, he saw a problem that impacted him deeply: "We drove over a dry river bed and there were people in the river bed digging holes and sticking their faces down into the holes," he recounted. "Our driver told me they were drinking. That was the first I had heard about communities that didn't have access to clean water and obviously it started a line of questions."

Haseltine started making the connection between the lack of water and the dramatic spike in HIV infections in Africa, where in 2001, five million adults and children were newly infected with HIV. Sadly, HIV/AIDS claimed the lives of three million people in 2001 alone. Haseltine connected the two issues, HIV and lack of clean water, and started brainstorming a possible solution.

That's when his observation of the problem turned into ownership of the problem. Upon their return from their mission trip, Jars of Clay founded Blood:Water. Their goal was to provide 1,000 African communities with safe drinking water.

Partnering with other musicians and activists, they raised enough money to provide clean water for more than 700,000 people in Africa and met their original target of 1,000 wells. As a result of their entrepreneurial approach, the communities with wells saw a decrease in stomach problems and skin diseases, and women and children didn't have to walk several miles a day carrying unclean water. Even those with HIV are stronger and are living longer.[4] None of that would have happened if, rather than take ownership and lead, Haseltine had deferred to someone else to figure out a solution.

3. Grayscale Thinking

Right or wrong. Good or bad. Yes or no. True or false. These binary responses may be helpful if you're an accountant or an electrician, but toggle-switch thinking is not going to solve problems if you're an entrepreneur. Conventional thinking shuts down creative solutions.

By contrast, grayscale thinking is all about applying an experimental mindset. This leads to finding a new way around a problem because you had the mental flexibility to find answers that were not obvious. Grayscale thinking, also known as integrative thinking, is your superpower. Entrepreneurs see and make indirect connections, often from an adjacent industry, and then take the risk of giving it a try.

"The consequences of integrative thinking and conventional thinking couldn't be more distinct," says University of Toronto professor Roger Martin. "Fundamentally, the conventional thinker prefers to accept the world just as it is, whereas the integrative thinker welcomes the challenge of shaping the world for the better."[5]

Jane Chen and her company, Embrace Innovations, provides a helpful example of grayscale thinking in action. I tell Chen's story in my book *The Vision Driven Leader*, but I'd like to recount it here. Globally, one in ten babies is born premature. Two of my granddaughters were preemies; the younger was born at just 27 weeks and weighed a little more than a pound. As you might expect, neonatal care is highly advanced in the developed world. But that's not so in undeveloped countries where preemies' chances are grim. In fact, about a million premature babies die each year, often because there's no reliable way to keep them warm.

Those figures shocked Chen, who in 2007 decided to tackle the problem as a class assignment. "No baby should die from being cold," she said. Using some pretty advanced tech, she and a team of fellow students developed the Embrace Warmer, a super-portable incubator that costs about $200. Armed with her vision of saving babies and her remarkable product, she launched her company, Embrace Innovations, to make it happen.

And this is where grayscale thinking became essential for Chen's success. Obstacles quickly emerged, especially with funding. She was reliant on donations and government contracts, which were unreliable and usually slow in coming.

She could have stuck it out, trying to make the most of her sponsors and partners. Or she could have thrown up her hands and said that working under such conditions was impossible. Instead, she figured out a way to stay on mission by generating her own funding.

Chen created a for-profit company called Little Lotus, selling swaddles, sleeping bags, and blankets with similar tech as her flagship Embrace Warmer. And she did it on the buy-one-give-one model popularized by Toms Shoes. "We thought, 'What if we could leverage our technology and create a product for the US market?'"

Starting a for-profit to self-fundraise for the non-profit was a successful step-around strategy that now helps fund the work overseas. As of 2017, according to a report in *Insights by Stanford Business*, Embrace Innovations "has saved more than 200,000 premature babies and hopes to increase that number to 1 million."[6]

4. Risk Tolerance

Entrepreneurs push against the norm. They understand getting to the other side of a problem requires taking numerous risks. Everything from time and capital to their health and reputation might be on the line.

What's more, failure—not just the risk of failure—is the one thing that all entrepreneurs have in common. "Failure is not an impediment to progress," as *The Economist* points out, "but is almost inevitably a requirement for success."[7] The willingness to shoulder risk and endure failure is directly connected to your ability to succeed.

Kathryn Minshew had a desire to make the job search easier and more efficient for job seekers and employers alike. At the time, the 25-year-old took a huge risk by abandoning her steady salary to shake up an already-established industry—online job search engines. Even after getting the business up and running, Minshew ran into roadblocks. A disagreement with her partners found her locked out of her site without her investment or her life savings—$20,000 total.

But that didn't stop Minshew. She founded what would become known as The Muse in 2011. Minshew had a vision to include content with her job search engine in order to create better matches for job seekers and employers. She was rejected 148 times when she pitched investors to finance her career website. The investors who rejected her insisted the concept wasn't scalable. Minshew experienced bouts of self-doubt and a lot of fear. But she persevered.

Today, it's the content feature that makes The Muse stand out and brings in more than 75 million users a year—most of them finding her website through the content before they ever actually search for a job. Since its founding, the company's workforce has increased four times over.[8]

In 2019, Minshew was one of the winners of the inaugural One Young World Entrepreneur of the Year Award. Minshew's willingness to take several risks despite several roadblocks is one of the reasons The Muse is so successful today.

5. Resilience

Resilience is the ability to rebound from failure. As entrepreneurs, we have to get comfortable with failure. We need to be able to bounce back when failure comes, especially when hitting a string of roadblocks, naysayers, or noes when we desperately need a yes!

How resilient are you intellectually? When you can't solve a problem, do you stick with it? Are you emotionally resilient when the door is slammed in your face by funders who dismiss your brilliant idea? How resilient are you when it's time to sell your company? Are you able to withstand tough negotiations, the deal falling apart, and then rebound for a greater win? Sabeer Bhatia did just that.

At age 19, he arrived in the United States from India to attend Caltech on a scholarship. He had $250 in his pocket. Upon graduation from Caltech and then from Stanford University with a master's degree in science, Bhatia worked for Firepower Systems. There, he befriended coworker Jack Smith. That's when Bhatia conceived an idea for a Web-based email solution called Hotmail. Partnering with Smith to launch Hotmail, they revolutionized email communication.

Wired magazine reports that Bhatia "built Hotmail's user base faster than any media company in history—faster than CNN, faster than America Online . . . signing up new users at a rate of 125,000 a day."

But their pathway to success required every ounce of resilience they could muster. Their back-of-the-napkin idea was rejected 100 times by investors until the Draper Fisher Jurvetson private equity firm stepped up with a $300,000 check. After the shock of finally securing funding, Bhatia reflected that they were just "two 27-year-old guys who had no experience with consumer products, who had never started a company, who had never managed anybody, who had no experience even in software—Jack and I were hardware engineers."

What Bhatia may have lacked in the way of a business plan or experience, he more than made up for with resilience. He said, "All we had was the idea. We didn't have a prototype or even a dummied graphical interface. I just sketched on his whiteboard."[9] Not only did he refuse to give up in the face of repeated rejection, Bhatia's resilience enabled him to stand his ground when it came time to sell the company.

In 1997, executives from Microsoft offered to buy the company for tens of millions of dollars. Bhatia refused to sell. Weeks later, after a series of intense negotiations, Microsoft raised their offer to $350 million. Against internal advice, Bhatia turned it down again. In the end, they sold Hotmail for a reported $400 million. Today, Hotmail is better known as Outlook.com.

Here's another reason resilience is so essential. Entrepreneurs lose more often than they win. For two decades the US Department of Commerce has conducted studies about how many new businesses fail. Currently about a million new businesses start every year. Here's the sad truth: 80 percent of the new businesses started in 2019 will fail within five years. Of those who do survive five years, 80 percent will ultimately fail. Put another way, 96 percent of new businesses today will not be operating ten years from now.

As RIM founder Mike Lazaridis points out, "What we have to remember is that trailblazers sometimes get lost. That's just what happens in unexplored territory. Research hits dead ends, promising avenues dry up, models collapse, people are just plain wrong. Over 90% of the time on the venture capitalist model you'd be losing your bet."[10]

Resilience matters because when entrepreneurs fail we need them to try again. If you stick with being open to solving problems long enough, you're going to have a substantial win. But only if you stay in the game.

6. Resourcefulness

Entrepreneurs are often scrappy, inventive types who find clever and unusual ways to overcome difficulties or make the most of opportunities. Unlike large corporations with big budgets, they have to identify and marshal whatever resources are on hand.

Down the road from where I live, a local entrepreneur opened a pizza shop in a small strip mall. At first, business was brisk as family and friends patronized the launch. While the road traffic in front of his store was high, sales proved to be softer than expected because a berm of tall trees obscured visibility. No one could see the shop from the road! Since the trees were owned by the retail complex, he couldn't just cut them down. He needed to find another way to increase visibility and foot traffic.

As is the case with most mom-and-pop business-es, he didn't have a lot of money to spend on marketing initiatives. And, even if he had marketing dollars, he knew the response rate to most direct marketing ini-tiatives might top out at just 2 percent. Hardly worth the spend. What he did have was a great pizza. He just needed to find a creative, cost-effective way to get people into his store.

That's when his partner suggested giving away a free pizza to everyone in the closest community. His idea was that one medium pizza would not be enough to feed a typical family of four, so they'd most like-ly buy another pizza—and, maybe breadsticks, salads, and drinks. They gave it a go.

They printed 300 photos of a pepperoni pizza on fourteen-inch round cardboard. The offer was straight-forward: Bring the cardboard pizza in and exchange it for a free, real one-topping medium pizza. They placed labels on the back of each promo piece so they'd know who claimed their free pizza. He used that informa-tion to build his mailing list.

During the afternoon, when business was typically

the slowest, he leveraged another resource at his disposal: his employees. They loved the guerilla marketing approach and gladly hung the pizza flyers on front doors. And it paid off. As dinnertime approached that evening, the phones lit up!

Care to guess the response rate on this direct marketing approach? Not the typical 2 percent. Not 10 percent. Not even 50 percent. A full 70 percent of the residents claimed their pizzas. And, as he had hoped, an overwhelming majority purchased additional items on the menu.

Giving away 210 pizzas at a cost of $3 each ($630), plus $100 in printing and labels, exemplifies resourcefulness. It also drove hundreds of new customers into his store. In fact, the approach worked so well that during the next several months they repeated the program in ten adjacent neighborhoods with similar results. (That's how I became a customer.)

7. Patience

Patience is sticking with a problem long enough to solve it. Patience is the ability to say, "This is what it's going to cost me now for the result I seek later—and I'll do what it takes to get to the end of the road." You remind yourself of your objective's importance, while tapping into your desire to succeed.

I developed this mindset when I was learning how to program my computer (back before they came ready to rock out of the box). I would sit there for 12 hours trying to solve a complex string of code. I'd try dozens of ways to get it right because I knew the payoff would be there if I just waited for it. Eventually, a few days later, I would have a fully functioning computer set up exactly as I needed it.

Patience includes the ability to have a long-term vision you're willing to invest in—even if it won't pay off for another two, three, even ten, or more years. Take someone who wants to get into the wine business. The process takes an enormous amount of time before you have anything to sell. After testing the soil, the vintner plants young vines on his raw land. He waters, prunes, and protects the vineyard from disease and pests, season after season.

After three long years, he's ready for the first harvest. But the first glass of wine is still a long way off. The wine must ferment, which takes a month, and then the aging stage begins, which can last from ten to sixteen months for Chardonnay, and upward of two years for Cabernet Sauvignon. Only then can the winemaker bottle the wine and reap the fruits of his labor. There are no shortcuts. But with patience there is reward.

8. Belief

Entrepreneur Jamie Siminoff had a problem. His wife Erin was aggravated every time she couldn't hear the doorbell when she was at the back of their house. Siminoff got busy. Believing his cell phone–connected, WiFi-enabled doorbell idea was the right solution, he raided his bank account and invented DoorBot. At the suggestion of a friend, Siminoff pitched his idea on ABC's *Shark Tank* (season 5).

With the exception of a lowball offer from Kevin O'Leary, all the sharks passed. Worse, Mark Cuban and Lori Greiner doubted the product's ability to connect with the market. Siminoff turned down "Mr. Wonderful" and his not-so-wonderful offer.

Afterward, Siminoff said he was in tears, because he was out of money and had faced so much rejection, he'd lost count of the rejections he'd received. But his unwavering belief in his solution drove him to rebrand and tweak the final product. Renamed RING, Siminoff's solution is now sold in more than 16,000 stores. He employees 1,300 people and his company is now valued at more than $1 billion.[11]

I've written at length about limiting beliefs over the years. Early in my career, I got stuck, not because I didn't have the money, time, skills, or contacts to make progress, but because of some deep-seated and wrong assumption about myself. For example, early on I thought I was too young to succeed. Now I routinely meet people who think they are too old to succeed.

Both views are flat wrong. Being young or old has very little to do with success. More often it's a lack of belief in ourselves that keeps us stuck. If you don't truly believe you're the right person for the task, find a different task before you risk your time and money. Look instead for opportunities where you believe you're the right person to meet the challenge.

Beyond believing in yourself, you have to believe in your solution. That belief will sustain you when, for example, you're making a pitch for funding. Pioneers like Siminoff can see a solution that has evaded others' observations. But those people don't and won't know that until the entrepreneur makes a convincing case. During the time it takes for them to believe in you, your belief in yourself and your solution is all you have.

Changing Definitions

At the beginning of the book I noted two definitions of an entrepreneur. The first is the classic definition, a businessowner. But the second is the more useful definition. It involves anyone actively risking something to bring a solution to those who need it. The traits we've reviewed here apply to the second definition.

In order to be that kind of entrepreneur, you don't necessarily need to own your own business. But you do need to be open, take ownership, exhibit grayscale thinking, tolerate risk, exercise resilience, be resourceful, exercise patience, and believe in yourself and your solutions. There's more to it, of course. There's also the method of entrepreneurialism. We'll cover that next.

4

———

THE SOLUTION FACTORY

Unpacking the Entrepreneurial Method

"Be glad when things don't work out as planned. You might just discover the next great invention." That sage advice, born out of personal experience, comes from Skip Yowell, cofounder of JanSport. When Yowell and his partner, Murray Pletz, designed their version of the perennial favorite A-frame canvas tent, they thought they had the best tent going.

Convinced they had a winner, they scheduled a showcase of their tent during a three-day, twenty-one-mile cross-country ski excursion in the dead of winter. The JanSport partners, two hippies with a love for the outdoors and modestly successful innovative frame-packs, invited several corporate executives from REI and a photographer from the *Seattle Times* to see their tent in action in Washington's Cascade Mountains near Blewett Pass.

On the first evening, the temperatures dropped to minus five degrees. The winds kicked into high gear and snow fell like crazy. Everyone scrambled to set up their tents, including the JanSport prototype. By three o'clock in the morning, after several hours of the storm's relentless pounding, their tent door zipper broke. The tent pole, which had previously secured the door, became dislodged and started to flail about like a propeller blade.

The tent was a colossal failure. Looking back on that fateful night, which Yowell considers "the worst night in our collective memories," he reflects,

> You might say we went to the mountain and returned with an epiphany of sorts. I mean, if the trip had been picture perfect, if the winds had behaved, if our newly designed A-frame tent had done its job, the inspiration for our Trail Dome tent might never have happened . . . Drawing upon our personal experiences in the field, as well as our failed attempt with the traditional tent approach, we brainstormed the idea of shaping a tent to resemble the Eskimo's igloo.

Yowell and Pletz set out to solve three things to better their failed prototype: the right design pattern, a better fabric, and a flexible pole system capable of supporting the dome in adverse wind conditions. Using readily available materials, they narrowed the pole options down to aluminum, solid fiberglass, and hollow fiberglass. Each option underwent intense testing, where the hollow aluminum pole emerged as the best.

At the time, the industry standard fabric was a cotton canvas blend that was bulky, heavy, easily developed holes and leaks, and often smelled musty—not to mention, the uninspiring color choice of either an army green or a drab dark blue. Yowell says they decided to go with a Dacron fabric "due to its exceptional strength and its ability to resist the sun's ultraviolet rays." In keeping with their hippie vibe, they chose bright orange and a sunny yellow. This new fabric became an industry game-changer.

One year after that fateful mountainside experience, JanSport was ready to go to market with their breakthrough dome tent. The backpacking community snapped them up. "We were so slammed with orders," Yowell said, "we had to sell tents on an allocation basis for many years because we could never make enough. This invention was the product that put JanSport on the map."

Their initial failure led to the hottest tent invention the camping industry had seen in decades. Mountaineers loved the superior, lightweight design. Day campers liked the ease of use. Looking back at what their entrepreneurial initiative accomplished, Yowell said, "To this day I carry with me a deep sense of satisfaction knowing that our groovy design forever changed the way the world camps."[1]

You probably noticed several traits of the entrepreneurial mindset in Yowell's story. His story also happens to highlight most of the eight stages of the entrepreneurial method. It's important to look at these in sequence for the same reason a golf player watches a video of their swing; by breaking it down and objectifying it, you cannot only understand it better but can also make it better. We'll take these one at a time.

1. Observe the Problem

Entrepreneurs are change agents with the finely tuned gift of observation. This relates to the openness we discussed in the last chapter. They observe when the presence—or absence—of something is creating friction or frustration for them or for their customers. This leads them to ask (and hopefully answer) two questions:

1. What does your customer want?

2. What's keeping them from getting what
   they want?

If you can identify and solve the "What's keeping them from getting what they want?" problem, you can make money. The entrepreneur's function is to help facilitate customer wants and expose other ways of doing things better, faster, smarter, more efficiently, or less expensively. That is to say, with less friction.

Take Red Rabbit founder Rhys Powell. Powell first came to the United States when he was 17 to attend MIT. He worked on Wall Street for a few years before deciding he wanted to do something that was more tangible and would help his community. His business idea came to him when a friend was complaining about how difficult it was to prepare healthy food for his daughter.

Powell began to research this issue and realized that no one was addressing how to get kids a variety of healthy food while at school. Parents were struggling and didn't have a lot of time. Powell hired a chef and nutritionist and got to work selling meals directly to the parents and delivering them to the schools. He spent $250,000 that first year and didn't make back any of his investment.

But Powell didn't give up. He knew this was a real need in his community, so he turned to the schools. In a *Forbes* interview, he reflects: "Coming from a computer science background, I didn't understand what it meant to feed someone. Food is how we build bonds with people."

Through the relationships he built that first year in business, he partnered with several private schools to bring in meals. He removed the friction of selling directly to the parents, which was cumbersome and expensive.

Following an angel investment, Powell was able to expand to low-income, public-school programs where he revolutionized again by keeping the same nutritional meal he was serving before at $5.50 but now at $3. Now Red Rabbit serves more than 100,000 meals a week to 165 charter and private schools in New York City and continues to grow rapidly.[2]

Friction can be anything that slows the customer down from making a purchase or completing a transaction. Customers will always follow the path of least resistance. If you want to generate more sales, you have to identify the friction points in your selling system and eliminate them.

When Amazon started doing business on the Internet, it had to overcome two major friction points. In the early days, when you made a purchase on the Web, you had to fill out your billing, shipping, and credit card information every single time. Customers didn't quite trust online retailers with their credit card information, and this friction point repeatedly reminded them that they were handing over their most sensitive information to complete strangers.

Then Amazon invented the one-click system. Customers entered their information once and then never had to think about it again. Buying an item was as simple as clicking a button. This made it easy for Amazon to capture impulse sales.

Another friction point was the shipping cost. Amazon had good discounts and a great selection. But by the time you added the shipping costs, it was often cheaper to buy the item from a local brick-and-mortar store. So, Amazon invented the Amazon Prime Membership. For a set annual fee, there are no individual shipping costs and a guaranteed two-day delivery. This eliminated their last barrier to impulse sales. The bottom line: less friction means more sales. The entrepreneur who innovates to remove friction from customer experiences will win. But that takes first observing the problem.

You can also make money and solve a consumer problem by observing how to help customers realize they want something they didn't know they needed. Take, for example, FedEx. Customers had a need to get stuff from point A to point B in a timely fashion. FedEx didn't create a new want, they just tapped into a current customer want at a deeper level, better than any existing solution.

It took the observation of Fred Smith, a Yale University student, to revolutionize the package delivery industry. Fred wrote an economics term paper on his concept of utilizing a computerized "spoke and hub" distribution system to offer overnight delivery.

His economics professor was nonplussed. "The concept is interesting and well-informed," he said, "but in order to earn better than a 'C', the idea must be feasible." That didn't stop Smith from launching his idea with his $4 million inheritance. He studied the air-freight industry, noted the flaws and deficiencies, and came up with an innovative and disruptive solution. Because FedEx added exceptional speed of delivery, they enhanced the customer experience. Need it tomorrow by 8:00 a.m.? FedEx can handle it.

By 2018, Smith's entrepreneurial hunch grew to a worldwide organization, serving 220 countries, generating $65.450 billion in US revenues, and creating 490,000 jobs.[3]

Entrepreneurs start by observing a problem and then thinking there must be a better way. If there's friction, the entrepreneur looks for a way to get around it. This leads to fresh innovation.

2. Aspire to Solve the Problem

Entrepreneurs don't just observe problems. They also have the desire to solve them. You may observe, for example, inefficiencies in the kitchen layout of your favorite coffee shop. An incredible solution might leap to mind, but you may not have any desire to solve that particular problem.

You may observe (and who doesn't) how unnecessarily complex the Federal Income Tax Code is. But even if you have a brilliant idea to radically simplify the process of reporting annual income, you might prefer a root canal to going down that path. (If you do aspire to be a change agent in that arena, go for it! You'll become a modern-day hero.)

You'll find yourself aspiring to find solutions to problems you've observed and that ignite your interest. You may think, *"I believe I could fix that"* or *"I've got an idea that might just work,"* or *"I've got a unique capability based on my existing skill set that could be leveraged here."* That's how I became involved in the productivity tools I've become known for and which helped launch Michael Hyatt & Company.

Whether it was solving problems with my

workflow, time management, email shortcuts, or finding the best productivity apps, technology, and the like, by scratching my own itch, I discovered solutions that worked for me. Then, when I observed other high achievers struggling with some of the same pain points, I aspired to help them by launching a blog to share what I had learned.

3. Visualize a Benefit

Remember the story of David and Goliath? King Saul and the Israelites were battling their archenemy, the Philistines. Each army was positioned on a hill with a valley separating them.

The Philistines had a formidable weapon: the giant Goliath. Standing almost ten feet tall, Goliath was one imposing warrior. His spear was almost three inches thick with an iron tip weighing fifteen pounds. Day after day, Goliath came out and taunted the Israelites, challenging them to send a man to battle him in hand-to-hand combat. If he won, Israel would become their subjects. If he lost, the Philistines would serve them.

Meanwhile, David was a young man at home taking care of his family's sheep. Early one morning, David's father sent him to the front lines with provisions for his brothers, who served in King Saul's army.

While he was there, Goliath emerged and shouted his challenge, as he had done for forty days straight. David overheard several Israelite soldiers talking about King Saul's reward for the man who would face Goliath.

They said, "Do you see how this man keeps coming out? He comes out to defy Israel. The king will give great wealth to the man who kills him. He will also give him his daughter in marriage and will exempt his family from taxes in Israel" (1 Samuel 17:25 NIV). This reward intrigued David. He was fixated on the benefits rather than on the (very tall) problem. Evidently David was confident he could take down the giant. If he did, he'd have a trifecta of benefits: great wealth, the king's daughter, and no taxes.

What's the connection to entrepreneurship? As you consider solving a problem, you know there will be a significant risk. In David's case, choosing to fight Goliath required him to risk his life, as well as the future of the Israelites. He had to be "all in."

Likewise, entrepreneurs know they're risking capital—perhaps mortgaging their home or spending their life's savings—to solve a problem. Who wouldn't want to know the rewards to determine whether or not the benefit is worth the risk? It could be that you're an entrepreneur in an organization staking your reputation on an innovation or initiative. On the upside, a promotion, a raise, a bonus, or some other perk awaits, including the pride or satisfaction that comes from solving a problem. On the downside, you could get reprimanded, reassigned, or even fired.

Visualizing the benefit is a clarifying moment. You have to ask, "Is the risk of my time, money, resources, and human capital worthy of the reward?" In light of the anticipated benefit, it's worth asking: What else could I do with my time and energy? After all, there's an opportunity cost. If you say yes to this project, you'll have to say no to other options—at least for now. Visualizing the benefits helps drive the decision whether or not to proceed.

4. Propose the Solution

After you've visualized the benefit of solving the problem, next, you should brainstorm and explore potential solutions to the given problem you're looking to answer. Part of this exploration takes into account identifying the current friction or pain points that the market is experiencing, as discussed above.

Cynthia Rubio saw friction firsthand season after season as hurricanes ripped through her Texas hometown and devastated entire states and Caribbean islands. Gearing up to return to the workforce following having her third child, Rubio was torn on what to do next. Her ultimate goal was to have her family spend more time together and have the flexibility to be with her kids during important events. She previously worked at Ford and considered doing real estate, but "realized I wanted to do something technical again," she says.

A friend suggested RFID-radio frequency identification, and Cynthia envisioned a new use for the technology, previously only used in shipping and tracking packages. She and her husband imagined wider applications, and in 2005 Radiant RFID made its debut at a business conference where 7,000 attendees had no need to stay in long lines for registration—instead, they were tracked by the RFID tags on their conference badges.

But Cynthia took the tracking technology a step further. Following Hurricane Katrina, Radiant RFID created the Special Needs Evacuation Tracking System to track storm victims and connect them with loved ones. It was first used during Hurricane Gustav and later during Hurricane Ike, successfully tracking 27,000 displaced storm victims.

Rubio identified friction in the marketplace, aspired to change it, and proposed a solution. She also yielded significant profit. Today, Radiant RFID continues to adapt and solve problems for tracking the world's most important assets, from people to cloud-based data files. And Cynthia solved her most important personal problem: she now has the family life she always wanted.[4]

5. Develop the Prototype

Now it's time to flesh out your idea and send it out into the world, at least partially. A prototype is an essential stage to gain real-world feedback. Depending on your product or service, the prototype should have the look and feel of what you envision, without necessarily being full-blown, final, or even functional. The idea is to refine the product and the user experience before committing significant dollars to the full execution and rollout.

In 2011, Payal Kadakia quit her day job to invest in her dance studio full-time. The decision gave her confidence to take an even bigger risk just a month later. After she spent the day struggling to find an open ballet class, she began to conceptualize what would become ClassPass.

Kadakia knew she was onto something and invested in a team. She and her team spent a year building out their app that allowed users to search classes at a variety of studios and gyms in one place. The initial launch didn't take off. The interface didn't click with users and utilization was slow. It took another year for the modern ClassPass to take shape—viewing and attending classes available at a variety of venues for one monthly fee.

By launching the initial app, Kadakia was able to gain critical feedback about user experiences. She was able to analyze the issues with her product, adjust, and improve. Learning from her customers, she developed a better version a year later—which is now valued at $1 billion. Today ClassPass has 30,000 studio and gym partners, 5 million classes available per month, and a presence in approximately 30 countries.[5]

Keep in mind there are different complexity levels when creating a prototype for feedback. A "quick and dirty" rendering could be as simple as a mockup, paper model, or set of drawings. If your idea is a new magazine, for instance, a digital mockup provides a representation of what you intend to make so that others can envision it, read it, and provide feedback. A more complex prototype, such as a 3D-printed model, will cost more but carries additional detail that is useful for those who will test it. And then there's a working prototype. While not the final product, it will have the bells and whistles you want the focus group or sales team to consider.

You can also try a minimal-viable-product release.

That's where you create an initial, scaled-down version of the product. If customers bite, you know you've got something. And you earned cash that might help produce and distribute the full-scale version. But just as important, you'll also get valuable feedback on what's working and what isn't. It's like doing R&D in public.

6. Test the Product

When you're about to take a prototype to market, you need to test every aspect you reasonably can. With testing comes revision. Numerous revisions are part of the process. As John Maxwell says, "Fail early, fail often, but fail forward."[6] In other words, failure in the testing phase is constructive when we learn from what went wrong and pivot toward the correct solution.

I find it helpful to remember failure at the testing stage is not an event. It's a process. The point of testing is to find ways to break the product. The time it doesn't break is when you know you're ready to launch. Thomas Edison understood that, having tried some 10,000 different ways to perfect the light bulb. He said, "I have not failed 10,000 times—I've successfully found 10,000 ways that will not work."

Rather than become hopelessly disheartened when working on prototypes that failed to pass the test, he said, "Many of life's failures are people who did not realize how close they were to success when they gave up."[7] That winning attitude needs to run deep at this stage because prototypes fail, fail, and fail again—until they succeed.

7. Iterate and Scale

Few innovations are perfect upon release. That's why, in virtually every computer, automobile, kitchen appliance, app, gadget, or widget, there are multiple editions or versions of the original offering. As the product "lives" in the marketplace, customer interaction becomes a source for further adjustments and innovation.

Think back to the Wright Brothers. Wilbur and Orville owned a little bike shop and, using their existing resources, developed the world's first "flying machine." Their maiden voyage on December 17, 1903, had a ground speed of about six miles per hour, an altitude of 10 feet, and carried one person all of 120 feet before touching down. It wasn't great, but it was a start.

The brothers went back to the drawing board to improve the design by streamlining the aerodynamics, perfecting the wings, and making adjustments to the propeller. Soon they were flying farther and higher than ever before. The US military became their first paying customer.

About four decades later, in 1947, other

entrepreneurs interested in air travel built the Bell X1 and broke the sound barrier with a rocket-engine-powered design. Two short decades later, on March 2, 1969, the Concorde made its maiden voyage flying with a top speed of Mach 2 (1,354 mph) with the capacity of carrying 128 passengers at an altitude of 60,000 feet. When the Wright Brothers first envisioned a man flying, they could not have anticipated just how much their invention would impact the world.

The same could be said of the automobile. Leonardo da Vinci, who created the early designs of what we now take for granted as the automobile, would be stunned at the all-electric, self-driving Tesla.[8] But that's how innovation by entrepreneurs works. They start with an initial concept, find a way to make it profitable, and, with time, competition enters the market and builds upon the innovation as new technologies emerge.

8. Benefit from the Invention

A key differentiator between rank-and-file employees and entrepreneurs is that the latter have a direct financial stake in the outcome. There's a line-of-sight connection between their efforts and their reward. Although not guaranteed, the prospect of an ultimate financial reward, bonus, or the sense of pride having completed the project drives the entrepreneur to navigate the myriad obstacles to reap their anticipated upside. They're solving problems for a profit. That's basic economics.

When the breakthrough comes, there's no shame in reaping the benefit of your labors. Rewards fuel entrepreneurs with an economic imperative to grow and grow more. Growth begets more growth. Most important, there's also a moral imperative because when you solve problems at a profit, you're making the world better for everybody through job creation and compounded economic growth.

I marvel at the economic impact sparked by the entrepreneurial "heroes" who started small and who now loom large, thanks to their creative endeavors. I have no idea how many of these successful businesses started at an entrepreneur's kitchen table or in the garage, workshop, dorm room, or apartment. An overwhelming majority of startups have humble beginnings. Just for fun, here's a short list of those who started with an idea and ended up benefiting from an international business:

- Amazon: Jeff Bezos, garage
- Apple: Steve Jobs, Steve Wozniak, bedroom
- Dell: Michael Dell, garage

- Disney: Walt and Roy Disney, garage

- FUBU: Daymond John, mom's house

- Google: Larry Page, Sergey Brin, garage

- Harley Davidson: William Harley, woodshed

- JanSport: Skip Yowell, Murray Pletz, transmission shop

- Nasty Gal: Sophia Amoruso, bedroom

- Lotus Cars: Anthony Colin, Bruce Chapman, stable

- Mattel: Harold Matson, Elliot Handler, garage

- Microsoft: Bill Gates, Paul Allen, garage

- Radiant RFID: Cynthia Rubio, kitchen table

- Softkey Software Products: Kevin O'Leary, basement

- Tatcha: Vicky Tsai, garage

- Wright Company: Orville and Wilbur Wright, bicycle shop

- Yankee Candles: Michael Kittredge, garage

These bold entrepreneurs invested long hours and their own funds to follow their dreams, while taking risks with no guarantee of success. Their entrepreneurialism, in turn, created economic value and jobs, launched or transformed entire industries. Any entrepreneur can follow in their footsteps. I hope many will.

As we saw in the last chapter entrepreneurship is a mindset. And this chapter reveals that it tends to follow a straightforward method. I'm convinced that anyone with the desire to do so can develop that mindset, follow that method, and make a contribution to the world.

While the contributions of Richard Branson, Elon Musk, and Bill Gates are legendary and dominate the headlines, in reality they're one piece of a whole pie. We can't afford to ignore the independent entrepreneurs also driving the economic growth we experience and depend on. Their work and innovation at the local dry cleaners, bakeries, coffee shops, juice bars, pizzerias, bookstores, farmer's markets, and so on are essential for the economy to thrive. They should rightfully benefit from their labors, especially given the risks.

Unexpected Winds

Let's go back to Skip Yowell's story. Yowell and his partner found themselves in about the most uncomfortable position any entrepreneur would want to experience. Imagine how they must have felt while the national tent buyer from REI watched their prototype fail spectacularly.

Did the shame of that dismal experience prevent them from trying again? No. They embraced their circumstance and allowed it to drive them forward to a completely different solution. Failure was just part of the process.

In fact, maybe we shouldn't even call it failure; feedback is a better term. By staying flexible, they were able to process that feedback and develop a new tent that disrupted and revolutionized the outdoors business for decades to come. And the truth is, as we'll see in the next chapter, entrepreneurs have to stay flexible when unexpected winds blow.

5

———

WHEN THE WINDS BLOW

A Pathway Through Crisis for Entrepreneurs

During times of crisis or disruption, entrepreneurs wonder: Should I pull back or lean in? Make drastic adjustments or hunker down? If their confidence isn't shaken, they probably haven't fully taken stock of what they're facing.

For example, in 2008, I was leading Thomas Nelson Publishers through the Great Recession. We were approximately a $250-million-a-year company with around 750 employees. It was a particularly frightening year. Nobody was using the word *recession* initially. We had some early warning signs as we noticed our sales slowing down, but we were also dealing with a couple of other industry disruptors.

First, we were trying to understand and address the transition to digital publishing from a physical publishing model. At the tip of this spear was Amazon's Kindle, released in 2008. That little device sent shockwaves through the publishing industry. No one knew if ebooks would be the wave of the future or just a short-term blip. We did know that digital delivery had gutted the music business—and publishers might be next. To hedge our bets, we immediately converted all print books to digital.

We also created a new process to produce every title simultaneously in both physical and digital formats. This required rapid renegotiations on author contracts because ebooks weren't covered in those agreements. New royalty structures needed to be vetted and applied.

On top of that, the social media revolution was changing our traditional marketing models. I felt like I needed to roll up my sleeves, get in there, and figure out for myself how to leverage social media for marketing our books. Existing marketing techniques needed to be adjusted. It was a big learning curve, but we began to see measurable success with utilizing social media to promote books.

As if ebooks and social media weren't enough,

another seismic shift was rattling our industry. Amazon had been rising to prominence for several years, changing forever the way readers discovered and purchased books. That led brick-and-mortar bookstores across the country to close their doors. It was while we were processing these new realities that the Great Recession hit.

It was a brutal time for me as a leader. The winds were blowing big time. But I knew that while being uncertain and afraid was normal, fear didn't have to define my response. When it became clear that the country was headed into a recession, I was able to strategically pivot not only personally in the face of the unknown, but also as a leader to maintain my confidence, make solid decisions, and find a way through.

Amazingly, Thomas Nelson remained profitable throughout the entire recession. We definitely had our challenges. We had to cut product lines and sales channels, as well as go through two rounds of layoffs. It was tough, but we made it through. Learning from successful entrepreneurs and reflecting on my own experiences, I've discovered a pathway for entrepreneurs working in times of crisis.

Recognize Your Situation

The first order of business is always taking accurate

stock of our present reality. Acknowledging the circumstances can be unnerving, even frightening—especially when the situation changes daily or when we're entering uncharted waters. But you can't ignore the facts or hide from reality.

It's always better to confront the facts when you can still do something about them. One of the most helpful concepts for that is called the Stockdale Paradox. I first read about it in Jim Collins's book, *Good to Great*. I've used it ever since.

Admiral James Stockdale was a prisoner of war for more than seven years in Vietnam. How did Stockdale endure? "You must never confuse faith that you will prevail in the end—which you can never afford to lose—with the discipline to confront the most brutal facts of your current reality, whatever they may be," Stockdale said.[1]

Based on the admiral's experience, Collins distinguished two aspects of getting through any hardship. First, recognize the most brutal facts of your current reality. Second, never lose faith that you're going to make it through in the end.

Entrepreneurs look for that golden mean, that middle way that recognizes hard realities but remains confident in the future. You can't take care of your business or anyone else if you don't take care of yourself.

If you sense yourself devolving to a place of panic, bring yourself back. One way to do that is to pay attention to your inputs. Recognize that you don't have control over what's happening in the world. You don't control the stock market's dips and spikes. You don't control the innovation by a competitor that may hurt your position in the market. However, you do have control over how you're thinking about the situation.

I find it helpful to recognize my emotions. Are they constructive or fearful? Are they empowering or destructive? Are they commensurate with reality, overblown, or conveniently evasive?

What we put into our brains is also key. That's why a heavy diet of news (I'm speaking from experience) creates a false sense of control. We believe that by being aware of what's going on, we have some control over it. But that's deceptive. A preoccupation with the news distracts from innovation and problem solving—the heart of entrepreneurship.

There needs to be a balance between staying informed and protecting your mental bandwidth. As a leader, if you're checking the headlines as part of a daily roundup, that's probably enough. More than that and you're going to infect your thinking. Your brain space needs to be focused on your purpose.

In times of uncertainty, it's especially important to remain connected to your vision. Proverbs 29:18 says, "Where there is no vision, the people perish"(KJV). Vision keeps us focused on the outcome—the destination. Vision is the *what*; strategy is the *how*. We want to stay committed to the vision but flexible on our strategy.

In a crisis, people have to be reminded of what we're fighting for. This is the "messy middle" where vision evaporates. Your words—speaking the vision—is the only thing that keeps it alive. This is also the antidote to fear. Remember: fear is contagious. But so is hope. Vision is what creates hope.

If you're fearful, the people around you will become fearful. People are counting on us to face the reality of our current situation. We can choose to lead confidently or hide in denial. Which one do you think builds credibility? Either our response will contribute to the crisis and fuel other people's fearful emotions, or we can respond with clarity and hope that we will prevail.

Reassess Your Position

Entrepreneurs have to take an honest appraisal of where they are so they can reassess. Quantifying any threats puts us in the best position to get our minds centered on what must be done to pivot and innovate. This process involves identifying vulnerabilities, looking for ways to mitigate risks, and taking advantage of opportunities.

Asking yourself questions like these can help you understand your possible exposure.

- Does the current situation pose a threat to any domains of my business?

- Are any supply chain disruptions likely or possible?

- What resources do I have that can be quickly repurposed or leveraged?

- How will my staff and customers be impacted?

- Will my marketing spend have to escalate or de-escalate?

- Are the right people in the right places to navigate what's on the horizon?

- How healthy are my reserves?

- What's my current cash position?

While identifying your vulnerabilities, I want you to imagine you own a restaurant. You may or may not. Either way it will serve as a fitting metaphor. The restaurant has four domains.

1. It has a **loading dock** where it receives the raw materials it uses to cook the meals it serves to its customers. This is the domain of your *suppliers*.

2. It has a **kitchen** where it prepares the meals. This is the domain of *operations*. This will be different in every business, but it is the realm of product development or client service you offer, along with all the necessary back-office support necessary to support those activities.

3. It has a **dining room** where it serves the meals. This is the domain of *customers*. This is the realm of sales, marketing, and customer service.

4. It operates in a **neighborhood** that indirectly has an impact on the restaurant. This is the domain of your business *environment*. This is the realm of critical infrastructure, government mandates, and even social environment. This is the stuff you can't control, but could have a big impact on your business.

After you have reassessed your vulnerabilities in these domains, you want to think about mitigating these newly exposed risks. For example, you might consider how you can reduce fixed costs, pause new expenses, and free up your time from obligations that are preventing you from innovating. Think through the possibilities of exiting an unprofitable business, cutting bureaucracy, or redeploying your staff who were working on things that are no longer relevant.

Everything should be part of your reassessment, including your product line. When Steve Jobs returned to Apple in 1997, he reassessed his new reality and learned that Apple's sales had dropped 36 percent between 1995 and 1997—from $11 billion to $7 billion. He also learned Apple was three short months from burning through their cash reserves. He immediately slashed the fat, cutting 70 percent of the product line. When asked why, he famously said, "Deciding what not to do is as important as deciding what to do. It's true for companies, and it's true for products."[2]

Likewise, when it comes to your customer base, ask yourself if there are clients you should let go. Some customers require enormous energy, time, and even money to remain happy. That drain on your resources isn't a good investment. No wonder Seth Godin encourages companies to fire "the 1 percent of their constituents that cause 95 percent of the pain."[3]

Every business leader operates in a unique context, so there isn't a perfect way to do this reassessment. I recommend a three-tier approach. Tier one is minimal but advantageous changes to your business. Tier two is a conservative rollback on your initiatives, perhaps redirecting resources to more profitable endeavors. Tier three includes radical moves like layoffs, renegotiating debt, and pivoting on your most significant products.

Look for New Opportunities

Once you reassess, you will have opportunities to make some strategic moves that will pay off not only in the current situation but also in the future. Ask the following questions to identify opportunities for your business:

- What do our current circumstances make possible?

- How are we uniquely placed to help customers right now?

- Do market conditions make our products suddenly more relevant?

- How can we make our products and services part of the solution that people need right now?

- What new partnership or alliance should we pursue to service clients?

You may uncover your team had untapped potential when they were realigned to new roles. You may discover ways of doing more with less or pivot with existing products and services. There could be products you want to get to market sooner or sales channels to add that you weren't considering before.

"The only thing we have to fear is fear itself." President Franklin Roosevelt said that during his 1933 Inaugural Address—smackdab in the Great Depression. It's still a good reminder today. What most of us don't know is the second part of that quote, where Roosevelt assured citizens that we need to be turning retreat into advance.[4]

During the beginning of the Great Recession, I was doing a lot of hand-wringing. I couldn't sleep. I had a hard time even eating. My flight-fight-freeze circuitry was activated, and I was viscerally feeling the fear.

In the midst, I met with my executive coach, Ilene. She asked me a question that changed everything for me: "What does this crisis make possible?"

That almost instantly pulled me out of fear and gave me hope. I shifted into the realm of possibility where creativity and innovation lay. What does a crisis make possible for you, your business, and your future?

For example, what can you do to sell more to your current customers?

- Can you lower the price or offer a discount?
- Can you extend payment terms?
- Can you make a buy-one-get-one-free offer?
- Can you pivot a product or service?
- Can you change your messaging to make your product or service more relevant?

In addition, are there new products you could bring to existing markets (or customers)? In a crisis, your existing customers have different needs.

- What do they need most to succeed?
- What do they need to avoid failure?
- What can you provide to make life easier for them?
- What do they need to overcome the new challenges they are facing?

There's always risk with new opportunities, but there's also the potential for great reward. Just consider the companies that started amid downturns and recessions: Hewlett-Packard (1939); Burger King (1953); Hyatt Hotels (1957); Trader Joe's (1958); Microsoft (1975); Apple (1976); CNN (1980); MTV (1981); Netflix (1997); Mailchimp (2001); Airbnb, Groupon (2008); Slack, Square, Uber, Venmo (2009); Instagram,

Warby Parker (2010).[5]

That's a partial list, but with those successes you could be forgiven for assuming all great businesses start in bad times. What about now? During the COVID-19 pandemic, virtually every state has had mandated stay-at-home and social-distancing policies. That has created a huge opportunity for companies like Instacart, Shipt, GrubHub, DoorDash, and other delivery services, and even sparked a renaissance of drive-in theaters. Could you reposition a product to address your current reality in a more palpable or obvious way for your customers?

This may be the most important work you do in a disruption. You *must* stay focused on opportunities so you don't cave into fear and paralysis. If something doesn't work, you have to pivot and try something else. That is the essence of resilience.

Shift your mindset from being reactive to being proactive so that you're in a mental space of abundance where you can create and innovate. In the face of reassessment, maintain your entrepreneurial spirit, and you will see new opportunities to make it through whatever crisis you find yourself in.

Respond with Action

We expect our military leaders to act and lead with

decisiveness. But two historic generals understood the word *action* very differently. General George McClellan was the leader of the Union armies during the Civil War, but he was slow to take action. He was so reluctant to fight that President Lincoln grew impatient and wrote him, famously pleading, "If you don't want to use the army, I should like to borrow it for a while." Not only did McClellan lose his job, but his inaction prolonged the war, costing the lives of tens of thousands of soldiers on both sides.

By contrast, General George Patton once said, "A good plan violently executed now is better than a perfect plan executed next week."[6] Patton is well known for his long and successful military career, especially several stunning campaigns in World War II. Our mindset should be to take action by doing the very best we can with what we have.

I understand the tendency to hesitate or try to calculate all the consequences of the decisions you're about to make. However, the surest way to fail as an entrepreneur is to hesitate, to hold back, to procrastinate decisions, to leave your customers and your team hanging. Dale Carnegie has famously put it this way: "Inaction breeds doubt and fear. Action breeds confidence and courage. If you want to conquer fear, do not sit home and think about it. Go out and get busy."

Resilience is an entrepreneur's superpower. You might be tempted to think, *"I wish I had more experience. I wish I had more cash in the bank. I wish I was smarter."* Who wouldn't want more experience, cash, or smarts? But there's nothing as helpful or as important as resilience, which I define as the ability to get knocked down and get back up.

US President Dwight Eisenhower, a former career Army General, once said, "Plans are useless but planning is everything." This points to the fact that planning and implementing are an iterative cycle. These are not once-and-done efforts. You'll likely need to pivot again. This will require additional planning as conditions on the ground change.

Make sure that you encourage your team to remain flexible and nimble. Build in the expectation that things are going to change. They shouldn't be surprised when they do. Having said that, to the extent you can, remind them of what's *not* going to change. This provides a "steady platform" from which they can metabolize the changes you are asking of them.

You and your team can't fail if you don't quit. If something doesn't work, try something else. If that doesn't work, use what you learned and pivot. Keep innovating, keep creating, and you'll get through to the other side. That's what entrepreneurs do over and over again. And it's why you, as an entrepreneur, are the best hope for our economy.

6

———

JOIN THE RESCUE

The Entrepreneurial Imperative

In May 1940 the future of Great Britain hung in the balance. The British Expeditionary Forces, along with French and Belgian troops, aligned themselves to stave off Adolf Hitler's advances in Northern France. But Hitler's armored and mechanized German forces outmatched the Allied forces who, in a standoff at Dunkirk, France, found themselves surrounded by the Germans.

With their backs to the sea, no room to retreat, and minimal means of communication, some 400,000 beleaguered British, French, and Belgian Allied troops were easy targets for Germany's intense air strikes. Without a miracle, annihilation was almost certain, and that most likely would have been the end of World War II. Hitler would have won.

With German forces controlling the territory around Dunkirk, the only remaining way of escape was a naval evacuation. There were two problems. First, the shallow coastal waters of the English Channel at Dunkirk barred Britain's Royal Navy destroyers from initiating a rescue. The closest their massive vessels could come to the shoreline was a mile out at sea. Second, the harbor was partially blocked by ships sunk from constant enemy air raids.

While the landlocked soldiers whispered prayers for deliverance, another battle of sorts was underway within the halls of Parliament. Having underestimated Hitler's ambitions and military might, Neville Chamberlain—who had previously maintained a position of appeasement toward Hitler—was losing the political support necessary to lead in a time of war. Chamberlain stepped down as prime minister on May 10. King George VI immediately appointed Winston Churchill to fill Chamberlain's shoes as prime minister as well as the minister of defense.

Churchill assessed the threat and understood what was at stake. Without an immediate rescue plan,

Britain's troops would be wiped out. Without an army, Britain would be defenseless—a sitting target for German onslaught. On May 19, Churchill enlisted Vice Admiral Bertram Ramsay to orchestrate a plan to salvage as many of the troops as possible.

Original estimates put the best-case number of lives saved by a sea evacuation at 40,000, about 10 percent of the troops. That wasn't acceptable to Churchill, nor to Ramsay. But within just five days, Ramsay devised a brilliant, yet unconventional, plan to save more troops by mobilizing a fleet of civilian boats to ferry the soldiers to the offshore battleships. These citizen sailors would enter a hot zone, facing threats from the inhospitable English Channel waters as well as air strikes from Nazi forces.

Ramsay put out a call over a BBC radio broadcast inviting anyone with a motorboat to assist with the evacuation. The response was incredible. A mishmash of 933 small, privately owned boats—sailing barges, yachts, merchant vessels, dinghies, fishing smacks, and cockle boats—answered the Royal Navy's call for help. Ramsay oversaw "the largest amphibious operation the world has ever seen."

This massive naval evacuation wasn't without casualties. Some 236 boats were lost to German air raids. But Ramsey's bold action rescued 338,226 troops, including 224,320 Britain Expeditionary Forces.[1] The little boats did what the large vessels could not. And that's true for entrepreneurs as well.

The Source of Growth

I sometimes think of the little boats of Dunkirk when I reflect on the importance of economic growth and the entrepreneurial role in the economy's health and vitality. The economist Wilhelm Röpke, whose policy recommendations were instrumental in Germany's post–World War II recovery, compared entrepreneurs to seafarers.

"The entrepreneur is like a ship's captain whose principal task is continuous navigation on the sea of the market, which is unpredictable because it depends on human nature," he wrote in his classic book, *A Humane Economy*. The eight traits we reviewed in chapter 3 are how entrepreneurs cope with that unpredictability. They're open, resilient, and resourceful, and the rest, because the seas might seem clear one moment and cloudy the next. It's easy to flounder without a mindset that keeps you even-keeled in a storm.

Röpke continued, "If a firm is to be successful and, in the degree of its success, discharge its economic function in society, it must be primarily oriented toward the market. . . ." The entrepreneurial method we covered in chapter 4 ensures, in Röpke's words, "The firm's face is turned outward, toward the market. . . ."[2] Why is that important? Because we must never forget that entrepreneurs serve a beneficial function in the economy and wider world. They are not fundamentally focused inward, but outward, to the market and to others.

The shame game is rigged. The idea that entrepreneurs take without giving is false. Entrepreneurs *make* and *give* more than most of us can fathom, especially as their contributions compound and grow over time and throughout the economy.

They are a creative force in the world, the link between needs and solutions. Without entrepreneurs, those needs go unmet and the society is poorer for it. But with entrepreneurs, needs are met, problems are solved, and the economy grows. And like the little boats of Dunkirk, entrepreneurs are the people best suited to accomplish this mission. And that's doubly true during times of economic crisis.

Time to Answer the Call

Economists and others have been raising concerns about economic stagnation and declining growth for some time now. See, for instance, Tyler Cowen's books, *The Great Stagnation* (2011) and *The Complacent Class*

(2017), or Robert Gordon's *The Rise and Fall of American Growth* (2016). The stock market in the last few years has been encouraging, but causes for concern persist, and that was before the novel coronavirus brought the world to a screeching halt.

I said at the start this book was a clarion call, not only a manual, but a manifesto. It's time to answer the call.

Entrepreneurs have a moral responsibility to respond to the crisis, like the little boats mustered for Dunkirk. Growth is a moral good. Failure to pursue our entrepreneurial vocation—in good times or bad—means we are failing to steward the unique gifts we've been given. In turn, we deprive others and jeopardize their futures because we've denied them life-benefiting products and services, income, financial security, and the compounding growth that those things create.

It's time to join the rescue. The world needs entrepreneurs. The world needs you.

APPENDIX 1

———

WHAT'S AGE GOT
TO DO WITH IT?

I want to pick up here on something I brought up in chapter 2, entrepreneurial age. Age should never be a disqualifier for entrepreneurs. Building a thriving economy requires millions of people investing their time, leveraging their talents, and contributing their unique insights—especially those shaped by experience.

I've been entrepreneurial my whole life, but the truth is I'm in my prime now and doing better work today than ever before. And data shows that's true for the majority of entrepreneurs. The reasons come down to one thing: resources. As a rule, we have acquired the resources we need to succeed as we enter our middle years. Think of it as an advantage in capital. Middle-aged and older entrepreneurs have more of the following key ingredients for a successful launch.

Life capital. It takes more than a great idea to run a company. Maturity and experience are major factors in decision making, team building, financial planning, and more. And there's no substitute for time spent in developing them.

Intellectual capital. More years means more knowledge. And because of age, this knowledge is fully integrated and intuitive. With age comes a better chance of seeing problems and finding solutions.

Social capital. Professional and personal relationships are critical for success, especially in today's economy. Older entrepreneurs have spent years investing in friendships and building their networks.

Financial capital. Money matters, and middle-aged entrepreneurs are more likely to have the capital to back their own ventures. Wadhwa tells the story of a 56-year-old who created an iPhone app that performs EKGs. He started his company with a quarter million of his own savings. Not many 25-year-olds can do that. This is especially important given the age discrimination in funding, mentioned in chapter 2.

I've written before about why retirement is a dirty word. When I was young, the dream was to retire at 50.

Now, I see these later years as the best years for creating new and exciting products, running high-growth businesses, and leveraging insights and strengths. Wadhwa put it this way: "The lesson here is that ideas come from need; understanding of need comes from experience; and experience comes with age."[1]

I'm not surprised to learn, according to research conducted by Dane Spangler for the Kauffman Foundation, that "in every single year from 1996 to 2007, Americans between the ages of 55 and 64 had a higher rate of entrepreneurial activity than those aged 20–34."[2]

What does this mean if you're middle-aged and older? If you feel like you're getting passed up by brilliant, fresh-faced kids with bright ideas, you're not. Be encouraged. Set big goals. And stay with it. Need inspiration? Look at these examples of later-in-life entrepreneurial endeavors:

- Auntie Anne's Pretzels: Anne Bieler rented a stand at a local farmer's market when she was 39 years old. With a ninth-grade education and no previous business experience, she had nine pretzel stands by the end of her first year. Her business has since been franchised and includes more than 1,000 stores and has sold over $375 million in soft pretzels.

- Huffington Post: Arianna Huffington founded the news site at age 55. It became the first commercially run American digital media enterprise to win a Pulitzer Prize. AOL acquired the site in 2011 for $315 million.

- BET Network: The first black billionaire, Robert Johnson, along with his wife, Sheila, were 34 and 31, respectively, when they founded the BET Network. Their goal with the network was to better appeal to African Americans. The company first turned a profit in 1985 and was the first black-owned business represented on the NYSE. Viacom bought the company for a record $3 billion, maintaining Johnson as CEO until 2006.

- GEICO: The company front man happens to be a Gecko. But the real genius was Leo Goodwin. At age 50, this corporate accountant identified a niche in the auto insurance industry and has since grown the company to more than 27,000 employees and 14 million policyholders.

- Denali Flavors: You might not have heard of them, but there's a high probability that their Moose Tracks ice cream is in your freezer. Founded by Wally Blume during his mid-50s,

Denali scoops up $80 million annually through their aggressive licensing program.

- Home Depot: Bernard Marcus got a pink slip from his hardware store employer Handy Dan. Unemployed, this ambitious 48-year-old along with former coworker Arthur Blank figured if you can't join 'em, fight 'em. Today their big orange lumber store has a net worth of $265 billion. Handy Dan went out of business in 1989.

- The Grommet: Jules Pieri founded the online marketplace for novel products when she was nearing age 50. Today the company generates more than $50 million in annual revenue and is responsible for launching brands such as Fitbit and SodaStream.

- INTEL: Robert Noyce had earned his physics doctorate from MIT, did the corporate gig for a number of years and then, at age 41, cofounded the company that today is the world's largest maker of semiconductor chips—worth an estimated $269 billion.

- LinkedIn: While not in his middle age, Reid Hoffman is, nonetheless, not part of the twentysomething class of entrepreneurs. At 35 years old, after the failed social networking platform, SocialNet, he launched the world's top networking platform for career-minded leaders.

- Martha Stewart Living: Martha Stewart was 56 years old when she leveraged her "own good taste into a multimillion-dollar business." She became the defacto lifestyle guru and has grown her net worth to $640 million.

- Mary Kay Cosmetics: Mary Kay Ash founded Beauty by Mary Kay when she was 45 years old after she was passed up for another promotion by a man she had trained. She built her company by investing in women and living out her principle of treating everyone with respect. Her company is now reported to have annual sales of $2.2 billion.

- McDonald's: 52-year-old Ray Kroc was schlepping milkshake machines with marginal success when he stumbled upon the McDonald's brothers. Kroc envisioned an opportunity to parley their processes into a national brand. After arriving at a somewhat controversial agreement, Kroc fueled an international juggernaut.

- Vera Wang: Vera Wang worked for *Vogue* magazine for 15 years and Ralph Lauren for

2 years before branching out on her own at age 40. She started with a boutique bridal shop and now runs one of the most recognizable fashion brands in the world, which brings in more than $43 million annually.

- Uncle Nearest: Already a successful real estate and restaurant entrepreneur and author, Fawn Weaver was stirred to a new venture at 40 after uncovering a problem at Jack Daniel's. The owners were evidently reluctant to honor the slave Nathan "Nearest" Green as the first master distiller. Weaver presented her research, demonstrating Green deserved the honor, but Jack Daniel's didn't act. So, she did. She launched her own whiskey company, Uncle Nearest, to honor a man whose recognition is long overdue.

And then there's Thomas Edison who founded General Electric at 45; Adolf Dassler, who launched Adidas at 48; Yoshisuke Aikawa, whose love of cars launched Nissan at age 52; Estee Lauder whose high-end brand of cosmetics was birthed at age 54; Amadeo Giannini, founder of Bank of America at age 60; and Charles Flint, who at age 61 founded IBM.[3]

If you are one of those brilliant kids with bright

ideas, stay humble and see what you can learn from middle-aged entrepreneurs about growing a business. Their perspective and personal experience can make all the difference to your future success.

If you're middle-aged or beyond, be inspired. Great things can happen as you lean into your God-given entrepreneurial spirit and unleash your creativity into a world that desperately craves your participation. It's time for young and old alike to kickstart the growth machine.

APPENDIX 2

———

HOW TO STAY HAPPILY MARRIED AS AN ENTREPRENEUR

If I had a dollar for every time people asked my wife, Gail, how she lives with an entrepreneur, I wouldn't have to be one. Scratch that. I would probably figure out how to get more people to ask the question. (Sorry, I can't help myself!)

Being an entrepreneur is part of who I am. And that creates some interesting challenges and opportunities in our marriage. If you are—or are married to—an entrepreneur, corporate executive, ministry leader, or any other kind of driven, "type A" personality, you know what I mean.

Gail and I approach marriage with a few basic assumptions: marriage attracts opposites; it takes work; it's a long-term project; and it works best when each party serves the other. The attraction is the easy part, isn't it? It's those other words—work, project, serve—where the challenges come in. But, like any good endeavor, that's also where we find the opportunities. So how can we work through the challenges and take advantage of the opportunities?

Gail and I have had over 40 years to work out the kinks. What we've discovered is that it comes down to an exchange of gifts. I'm not talking jewelry and surprise vacations. There's nothing wrong with those, but I'm talking about something far more valuable. There are five gifts each partner can give to the other to help build a happy marriage.

It's important to say at the outset that these lists are not gendered in any way. Gail and I have a fairly traditional marriage, but these gifts work with just about any arrangement of an entrepreneur and their spouse.

5 Gifts from Entrepreneurs to Their Spouses

A great marriage requires investment from both parties. So how do entrepreneurs achieve their dreams without sabotaging their marriage in the process? If you are the entrepreneur in your marriage, you can help your spouse (and yourself) by giving him or her these five gifts:

- *The gift of honor.* Our spouses are more important than our work, whatever that work may be. To give this gift, we esteem and value what our spouses esteem and value. We give priority to their priorities, and use our words to praise and uplift, especially when our spouses are absent.

- *The gift of awareness.* It's easy in the hyper focus of hard-drivers to see themselves as the center of the show. We're not—no matter how much money we make. We need to be aware of all the material and nonmaterial contributions our spouses make to our lives.

- *The gift of inclusion.* Including our spouses in our businesses creates intimacy, builds trust, and brings us together. Whether it's just receiving input or counsel, or getting into the nitty-gritty details of the business, our marriages win if we keep our spouses in the loop.

- *The gift of commitment.* Given the risk inherent to the entrepreneurial lifestyle, some of

the most important words we can hear are,
"We're in this together, no matter what."
Communicating that kind of commitment can
get a couple through almost anything.

- *The gift of trust.* Because the entrepreneurial
  life is risky, it's easy to default to fear. So
  many things can go wrong. To counter that,
  we can easily overwork. That ends up taking,
  not giving. Instead, we can bless our spouses
  by realizing it doesn't all hang on our solitary
  shoulders.

That's half the picture. What about the other set of
gifts?

5 Gifts from Spouses to Entrepreneurs

If you are married to an entrepreneur, you can help
him or her (and yourself) by giving these five gifts.
Gail came up with this list. I would characterize these
as gifts of support:

- *The gift of belief.* There is a lot of risk in
  the entrepreneurial life. I'm someone who
  struggles with fear and doubt, and it makes all
  the difference for Gail to say, "You have what
  it takes"—especially when I lose sight of that
  myself.

- *The gift of appreciation.* Facing all that risk can be taxing. But when I see my sacrifices are appreciated, it lights my fire. Gratitude from Gail motivates me like nothing else. It also makes me deeply grateful for her.

- *The gift of affirmation.* The entrepreneurial lifestyle involves long hours, sometimes away from home. It would be easy for Gail to go negative. But by affirming what she loves about me—those things that attracted her in the first place—it enables both of us to stay positive. And that means when we have to have tough conversations, we have the relational equity we need to grow, not crumble.

- *The gift of perspective.* The intense focus of entrepreneurs enables massive creativity and achievement, but it can come at the cost of perspective. I can easily think that everything in my world rises or falls with the next project. Gail keeps the wide angle I sometimes lose.

- *The gift of commitment.* We talked about this in the previous list. But this is an essential gift for both spouses to give and receive. It's critical to make this commitment concrete and observable in our actions.

I've received all of these gifts in abundance from Gail. And I'm convinced I wouldn't have the resources I need without them. They are a huge part of my success—even my sanity.

The numbers I've seen on divorce among entrepreneurs and executives is sobering. But having a happy marriage and an entrepreneurial career is possible.

These simple but priceless gifts have seen Gail and me through more than four decades of marriage so far. We've never been perfect, but our marriage has never been better. I believe it's possible to accomplish your entrepreneurial dreams without blowing up your marriage. Better than that, I also believe you can have a great marriage if you're intentional and generous.

ABOUT THE AUTHOR

———

Michael Hyatt is the founder and CEO of Michael Hyatt & Company, which helps leaders get the focus they need to win at work *and* succeed at life. Formerly chairman and CEO of Thomas Nelson Publishers, Michael is also the creator of the *Full Focus Planner* and a *New York Times*, *Wall Street Journal*, and *USA Today* bestselling author of several books, including *Free to Focus*, *Your Best Year Ever*, *Living Forward*, and *Platform*. His work has been featured by the *Wall Street Journal*, *Forbes*, *Inc.*, *Fast Company*, *Businessweek*, *Entrepreneur*, and other publications. Michael has been married to his wife, Gail, for more than forty years. They have five daughters, three sons-in-law, and nine grandchildren. They live just outside Nashville, Tennessee. Learn more at MichaelHyatt.com.

NOTES

CHAPTER 1: WHO NEEDS ENTREPRENEURS?

1   Michael R. Strain, "The Right Is Wrong to Lose Faith in Economic Growth," *Bloomberg Quint*, November 23, 2018, https://www.bloombergquint.com/view/right-wing-populists-are-wrong-about-economic-growth.

2   Tyler Cowen, *Stubborn Attachments* (San Francisco: Stripe, 2018), 40.

3   Zoltan Acs, "How Is Entrepreneurship Good for Economic Growth?" *Innovations*, Winter 2006, https://www.mitpressjournals.org/doi/pdf/10.1162/itgg.2006.1.1.97.

4   Rich Cooper, "Why Are We Shaming America's Entrepreneurs?" US Chamber of Commerce Foundation, March 10, 2014, https://www.uschamberfoundation.org/blog/post/why-are-we-shaming-america-s-entrepreneurs/34128.

5   Gene Marks, "Why Small Business Owners Should Fear the Sanders and Warren Tax Plans," *The Hill*, October 2, 2019, https://thehill.com/opinion/finance/464048-why-small-business-owners-should-fear-the-sanders-and-warren-tax-plans.

6   "Small Businesses Generate 44 Percent of U.S. Economic Activity," US Small Business Administration Office of Advocacy, January 30, 2019, https://advocacy.sba.gov/2019/01/30/small-businesses-generate-44-percent-of-u-s-economic-activity.

7   Ray Hennessey, "Why Americans Don't Want to Start New Businesses," *Entrepreneur*, May 7, 2014, https://www.entrepreneur.com/article/233689.

CHAPTER 2: THEY'RE DISAPPEARING

1   Derek Thompson, "The Mysterious Death of Entrepreneurship in America," *The Atlantic*, May 12, 2014, https://www.theatlantic.com/business/archive/2014/05/entrepreneurship-in-america-is-dying-wait-what-does-that-actually-mean/362097. Edward C. Prescott and Lee E. Ohanian, "Behind the Productivity Plunge: Fewer Startups," *Wall Street Journal*, June 25, 2014, https://www.wsj.com/articles/behind-the-productivity-plunge-fewer-start-ups-1403737197. Stephen Harrison, "Start-Ups Aren't Cool Anymore," *The Atlantic*, December 5, 2018, https://www.theatlantic.com/business/archive/2018/12/millennial-start-up/567793. Leigh Buchanan, "American Entrepreneurship Is Actually Vanishing. Here's Why," *Inc.*, May 2015, https://www.inc.com/magazine/201505/leigh-buchanan/the-vanishing-startups-in-decline.html. Noah Smith, "America's Startup Scene Is Looking Anemic," Bloomberg.com, June 7, 2018, https://www.bloomberg.com/opinion/articles/2018-06-07/america-s-startup-scene-is-looking-anemic. Dan Kopf, "The US Startup Is Disappearing," *Quartz*, June 20, 2018, https://qz.com/1309824/the-us-startup-company-is-disappearing-and-thats-bad-for-the-economy. "Dynamism in Retreat," Economic Innovation Group, February 2017, https://eig.org/dynamism.

2   Buchanan, "American Entrepreneurship Is Actually Vanishing."

3   Wim Naudé, "The Surprising Decline of Entrepreneurship and Innovation in the West," *The Conversation*, October 8, 2019, https://theconversation.com/the-surprising-decline-of-entrepreneurship-and-innovation-in-the-west-124552.

4   Paula Nagler and Wim Naudé, "How Germany's Declining Innovativeness Contributes to Inequality," GEDProject.de, August 8, 2018, https://ged-project.de/digitization-and-innovation/how-germanys-weak-innovation-eco-system-is-driving-inequality. Andrew R. Karlin, "The Entrepreneurship Vacuum in Japan: Why It Matters and How to Address It," Wharton University of Pennsylvania, January 2, 2013, https://knowledge.wharton.upenn.edu/article/the-entrepreneurship-vacuum-in-japan-why-it-matters-and-how-to-ad-

dress-it. "How to Rev Up Japanese Startups," *Economist*, November 5, 2016, https://www.economist.com/business/2016/11/05/how-to-rev-up-japanese-startups. "Entrepreneurship in Canada," Grant-Thornton.ca, December 19, 2018, https://www.grantthornton.ca/insights/entrepreneurship-in-canada. Ryan Macdonald, "Business Entry and Exit Rates in Canada: A 30-Year Perspective," Statistics Canada, November 27, 2015, https://www150.statcan.gc.ca/n1/pub/11-626-x/11-626-x2014038-eng.htm. "Why Fewer South Africans Want to Start Their Own Businesses," *BusinessTech*, May 18, 2017, https://businesstech.co.za/news/business/175765/why-fewer-south-africans-want-to-start-their-own-businesses/. Yulia Krylova, *Corruption and the Russian Economy* (New York: Routledge, 2018), Wim Naudé, "Is European Entrepreneurship in Crisis?" IZA Discussion Paper, No. 9817, March 2016, https://papers.ssrn.com/sol3/papers.cfm?abstract_id=2750300. "Les Misérables," *Economist*, July 28, 2012, https://www.economist.com/briefing/2012/07/28/les-miserables.

5   Ben Casselman, "A Start-Up Slump Is a Drag on the Economy. Big Business May Be to Blame," *New York Times*, September 20, 2017, https://www.nytimes.com/2017/09/20/business/economy/start-up-business.html.

6   Hennessey, "Why Americans Don't Want to Start New Businesses."

7   "Studies on Barriers to Entrepreneurship," Institute for Justice, accessed August 8, 2020, https://ij.org/research-types/studies-on-barriers-to-entrepreneurship.

8   Beth Kregor, "Regulatory Field," Institute for Justice, November 2010, https://ij.org/report/regulatory-field.

9   Scott A. Shane, "Are We Becoming Less Entrepreneurial?" *You're the Boss* (blog) *New York Times*, June 30, 2009, https://boss.blogs.nytimes.com/2009/06/30/are-we-becoming-less-entrepreneurial. Casselman, "A Start-Up Slump Is a Drag on the Economy."

10 Chris Ducker, "Why You—Yes, You!—Should Be an Entrepreneur," *MichaelHyatt.com*, March 20, 2018, https://michaelhyatt.com/you-should-be-an-entrepreneur/.

11 Buchanan, "American Entrepreneurship Is Actually Vanishing."

12   Craig Hall, "How the Decline in Community Banks Has Hurt U.S. Entrepreneurship," *Barrons.com*, May 18, 2019, https://www.barrons .com/articles/how-the-decline-in-community-banks-has-hurt-u-s-entrepreneurship-51558184413.

13   "We Ask: What's Your Biggest Challenge? Entrepreneurs Say: It's Financing," *CO—*, February 25, 2019, https://www.uschamber.com/ co/run/business-financing/business-financing-challenges.

14   Dave Lavinsky, "First-Time Entrepreneurs' Biggest Mistake? Lack of Capital," *Christian Science Monitor*, October 26, 2012, https://www.csmonitor.com/Business/new-economy/2012/1026/ First-time-entrepreneurs-biggest-mistake-Lack-of-capital.

15   Buchanan, "American Entrepreneurship Is Actually Vanishing. Here's Why."

16   Arnobio Morelix, Victor Hwang, Inara S. Tareque, "Zero Barriers," Kauffman Foundation, 2017, https://www.kauffman.org/wp-content/uploads/2020/04/state_of_entrepreneurship_address_report_2017.pdf.

17   Sean Geng, "Do You Have What It Takes to Be a Successful Millennial Entrepreneur?" *Inc.*, December 13, 2017, https://www .inc.com/young-entrepreneur-council/5-factors-that-help-millennial-entrepreneurs-succeed.html.

18   Ruth Simon and Caelainn Barr, "Endangered Species: Young U.S. Entrepreneurs," *Wall Street Journal*, January 2, 2015, https:// www.wsj.com/articles/endangered-species-young-u-s-entrepreneurs-1420246116.

19   "State of Startups: 2018," First Round, https://stateofstartups .firstround.com/2018/#ageism-in-tech.

20   Nathaniel Rich, "Silicon Valley's Start-Up Machine," *New York Times Magazine*, May 2, 2013, https://www.nytimes .com/2013/05/05/magazine/y-combinator-silicon-valleys-start-up-machine.html.

21   Vivek Wadhwa, "The Truth About Entrepreneurs: Twice as Many Are Over 50 as Are Under 25," *PBS News Hour*, April 26, 2013, https://www.pbs.org/newshour/economy/the-truth-about-entrepre-

neurs-twice-as-many-are-over-50-than-under-25. Vivek Wadhwa, "Why Middle-Aged Entrepreneurs Will Be Critical to the Next Trillion-Dollar Business," VentureBeat, October 31, 2014, https://venturebeat.com/2014/10/31/why-middle-aged-entrepreneurs-will-be-critical-to-the-next-trillion-dollar-business/.

22   Amy Felegy, "About-Face: Making Masks Across the Community," *SW News Media*, April 2, 2020, https://www.swnewsmedia.com/chaska_herald/news/business/about-face-making-masks-across-the-community/article_3e60e82f-f152-5ecf-b9b4-5848e99ceb17.html.

CHAPTER 3: A BETTER WAY

1   Brent Schlender and Rick Tetzeli, *Becoming Steve Jobs* (New York: Crown Business, 2015), 408.

2   Israel M. Kirzner, *Competition and Entrepreneurship* (Chicago: University of Chicago Press, 1978), 41.

3   Robyn Williams, "Mike Lazaridis: The Power of Ideas," ABC.net .au, June 9, 2012, https://www.abc.net.au/radionational/programs/scienceshow/mike-lazaridis——the-power-of-ideas/4053180.

4   Thomas Goliber, "The Status of the HIV/AIDS Epidemic in Sub-Saharan Africa," PBR.org, July 2, 2002, https://www.prb .org/thestatusofthehivaidsepidemicinsubsaharanafrica/. Associated Press, "Jars of Clay Completes 1,000 Wells Project," Syracuse.com, March 22, 2019, https://www.syracuse.com/entertainment/2010/12/jars_of_clay_completes_1000_we.html. "The History of Blood: Water Mission," Blood:Water Mission, https://www.bloodwater.org/mission-history.

5   Roger L. Martin, "How Successful Leaders Think," *Harvard Business Review*, June 2007, https://hbr.org/2007/06/how-successful-leaders-think.

6   Jennifer Luna, "Jane Chen: Be Courageous Because You Will Fail," Insights by Stanford Business, July 31, 2017, https://www.gsb .stanford.edu/insights/jane-chen-be-courageous-because-you-will-fail. See also: Karen Weise, "Jane Chen: A Simple, Effective Way to Reduce Infant Mortality, *Bloomberg Business Week*, April 11, 2016, https://www.bloomberg.com/features/2016-design/a/jane-chen.

7   Laura Montgomery, "Entrepreneurial Thinking: The Key to Corporate Survival," *Economist*, accessed June 10, 2020, https://exed.economist.com/career-advice/industry-trends/entrepreneurial-thinking-key-corporate-survival.

8   Vivian Giang, "11 Famous Entrepreneurs Share How They Overcame Their Biggest Failure," *Fast Company*, May 4, 2014, https://www.fastcompany.com/3029883/11-famous-entrepreneurs-share-how-they-overcame-their-biggest-failure.

9   Jeremy Gutsche, *Create the Future* (New York: Fast Company Press, 2020), 19. Po Bronson, "HotMale," *Wired.com*, December 1, 1998, https://www.wired.com/1998/12/hotmale.

10   Williams, "Mike Lazaridis: The Power of Ideas."

11   Ali Montag, "This $1 Billion Company Was Once Rejected on 'Shark Tank'—Here's How the Founder Proved Everyone Wrong," CNBC.com, November 30, 2017, https://www.cnbc.com/2017/11/30/shark-tank-reject-doorbot-is-now-billion-dollar-company-ring.html. Alejandro Cremades, "These Entrepreneurs Were Rejected Hundreds of Times Before Bringing in Billions," *Forbes*, February 5, 2019, https://www.forbes.com/sites/alejandrocremades/2019/02/05/these-entrepreneurs-were-rejected-hundreds-of-times-before-bringing-in-billions/#2b676e0e5c67.

CHAPTER 4: THE SOLUTION MACHINE

1   Skip Yowell, *The Hippie Guide to Climbing the Corporate Ladder and Other Mountains* (Nashville: Thomas Nelson, 2006).

2   Susan Adams, "At Red Rabbit, a Former Wall Street Trader Tries to Make a Profit Selling Healthy School Lunches," *Forbes*, November 30, 2016, https://www.forbes.com/sites/forbestreptalks/2016/11/30/at-red-rabbit-a-former-wall-street-trader-tries-to-make-a-profit-selling-healthy-school-lunches/#49e7877d72f3.

3   "Fred Smith: An Overnight Success," *Entrepreneur.com*, October 9, 2008, https://www.entrepreneur.com/article/197542. "FedEx 2018 Form 10-K Annual Report," *U.S. Securities and Exchange Commission,* July 16, 2018, https://www.sec.gov/Archives/edgar/data/1048911/000119312514267851/d752614d10k.htm. About Us,

"Connecting People & Possibilities," *FedEx.com*, accessed May 30, 2020, https://www.fedex.com/en-us/about.html.

4   Gail Cameron Wescott, "How Cynthia Rubio Turned an Idea into a Million Dollar Business," *Reader's Digest*, December 5, 2008, updated April 6, 2020, https://www.rd.com/article/how-cynthia-rubio-turned-an-idea-into-a-million-dollar-business/.

5   Megan DiTrolio, "Payal Kadakia Made ClassPass into the Decade's First Billion-Dollar Company," *Marie Claire*, March 5, 2020, https://www.marieclaire.com/career-advice/a31138885/payal-kadakia-classpass-billion-dollar-company.

6   John C. Maxwell, *Failing Forward* (Nashville: Thomas Nelson, 2000), 114.

7   Erica R. Hendry, "7 Epic Fails Brought to You by the Genius Mind of Thomas Edison," *Smithsonian Magazine*, November 20, 2013, https://www.smithsonianmag.com/innovation/7-epic-fails-brought-to-you-by-the-genius-mind-of-thomas-edison-180947786/. "Forbes Quotes: Thoughts on the Business of Life," *Forbes*, accessed May 30, 2020, https://www.forbes.com/quotes/8999/.

8   Rossella Lorenzi, "Da Vinci Sketched an Early Car," Australian Broadcast Corporation, April 26, 2004, http://www.abc.net.au/science/news/stories/s1094767.htm.

CHAPTER 5: WHEN THE WINDS BLOW

1   James C. Collins, *Good to Great* (New York: HarperCollins, 2001), 85.

2   Connie Guglielmo, "A Steve Jobs Moment That Mattered: *Macworld*, August 1997," *Forbes*, October 7, 2012, https://www.forbes.com/sites/connieguglielmo/2012/10/07/a-steve-jobs-moment-that-mattered-macworld-august-1997/#574204753edd. Nick Whigham, "The Forgotten Microsoft Deal That Saved Apple from Bankruptcy," *News.com*, August 5, 2018, https://www.news.com.au/technology/gadgets/the-forgotten-microsoft-deal-that-saved-apple-from-bankruptcy/news-story/b5bf0262c42cf0ceeef2c9438dcf1ed0. Walter Isaacson, "The Real Leadership Lessons of Steve Jobs," *Harvard Business Review*, April 2012, https://hbr.org/2012/04/the-real-leadership-lessons-of-steve-jobs.

3   Seth Godin, "The Customer Is Always Right," *Seth's Blog*, April 28, 2006, https://seths.blog/2006/04/the_customer_is/.

4   Franklin D. Roosevelt, Inaugural Address, March 4, 1933, whitehouse.gov, https://www.whitehouse.gov/about-the-white-house/presidents/franklin-d-roosevelt/.

5   Darren Dahl, "Top Companies Started During a Recession," *HuffPost*, August 11, 2011, https://www.huffpost.com/entry/top-companies-started-during-a-recession_n_923853. Matthew Wilson, "14 Successful Companies That Started During US Recessions," *Business Insider*, April 20, 2020, https://www.businessinsider.com/successful-companies-started-during-past-us-recessions-2020-4. Annisha, "12 Businesses That Started During a Recession," *Looka*, April 14, 2020, https://looka.com/blog/businesses-that-started-during-a-recession. Audrey Conklin, "10 Successful startups Founded During 2008 Great Recession," FoxNews.com, March 29, 2020, https://www.foxbusiness.com/markets/startups-great-recession.

6   Alan Axelrod, *Patton's Drive* (Guilford, CT: Lyons Press, 2009), 39.

CHAPTER 6: JOIN THE RESCUE

1   John Hayes Fisher, Dan Gold, David McNab, and Dan Chambers, "Great Escape at Dunkirk," PBS.org, February 14, 2018, https://www.pbs.org/wgbh/nova/video/great-escape-at-dunkirk. The Newsroom, "Forgotten Scottish Admiral Who Saved Britain at Dunkirk," *Scotsman*, July 30, 2017, https://www.scotsman.com/news/politics/forgotten-scottish-admiral-who-saved-britain-dunkirk-1444031. "Operation Dynamo: Things You Need to Know About the Dunkirk Evacuation," English Heritage, https://www.english-heritage.org.uk/visit/places/dover-castle/history-and-stories/operation-dynamo-things-you-need-to-know.

2   Wilhelm Röpke, *A Humane Economy*, translated by Elizabeth Henderson (Indianapolis: Liberty Fund, 1971), 255.

APPENDIX 1: WHAT'S AGE GOT TO DO WITH IT?

1   Wadhwa, "The Truth About Entrepreneurs."

2   Scott Shane, "Entrepreneurship Is a Midlife Game," *Entrepreneur*, February 15, 2013, https://www.entrepreneur.com/article/225843.

3   "Too Late to Start? Life Crisis and Late Bloomers—Infographic," *Adioma.com*, August 13, 2014, https://blog.adioma.com/too-late-to-start-life-crisis-infographic.

INDEX